I. P Hughlings

The Logic of Names

An Introduction to Boole's Laws of Thought

I. P Hughlings

The Logic of Names
An Introduction to Boole's Laws of Thought

ISBN/EAN: 9783744675420

Printed in Europe, USA, Canada, Australia, Japan

Cover: Foto ©Thomas Meinert / pixelio.de

More available books at **www.hansebooks.com**

THE LOGIC OF NAMES.

AN INTRODUCTION

TO

BOOLE'S LAWS OF THOUGHT.

BY

I. P. HUGHLINGS.

———◆———

"The symbolic language of Algebra, framed wholly on notions of number and quantity, is adequate, by what is certainly not an accident, to the representation of all the laws of thought."—DE MORGAN.

———◆———

LONDON:

JAMES WALTON, 137, GOWER STREET.

—

1869.

LONDON :
PRINTED BY WERTHEIMER, LEA AND CO.,
FINSBURY CIRCUS.

CONTENTS.

ADVERTISEMENT.

PRIMARILY these pages are an attempt to independently think out and popularly interpret some of the principles characteristic of Mr. John Stuart Mill's Logic, of the late Professor Boole's Laws of Thought, and of Mr. De Morgan's various publications on the same class of subjects.

The following special objects have been aimed at :—

1st. To, so far as possible, divest of their mathematical dress the foundations of Professor Boole's theory.

2nd. To independently and popularly expound and interpret these foundations.

3rd. To include in this exposition some account of certain phrases and doctrines which have been taken and adopted from the logic of the past by common language and general literature.

I. P. H.

THE LOGIC OF NAMES.

INTRODUCTION.—Man is a result of the operation of forces, some of which are known, and
some unknown; the former subjects of knowledge, the latter subjects of belief. To the
unknown we give the name of Soul; those that
are known we refer either to Mind or to Body.
By the distinction of Mind and Body is not
necessarily implied that between material and
immaterial. The immaterial we refer to the
unknown, to what is subject of belief; but the material each man divides for himself into that which
he cannot separate from his own individuality,
and that which he can so separate. Such a distinction is manifestly both ambiguous and fluctuating. It is ambiguous, because it may be understood in two senses. We may draw the dividing
line through different systems of points. It is
fluctuating, because, wherever placed in the first
instance, no subsequent tracing will repeat it. The
line may be drawn so as to separate all the matter
which composes the individual's body from other
matter. Such a line is uncertain to the kitten,
which runs after its own tail, and to the human

B

being who, applying crossed fingers to the tip of his nose, imagines for an infinitesimal portion of time that he has two noses. A cultivated man attempts to draw the line so as to include the thinking part of his material frame only. Or, rather, he assumes the line to be drawn, and calls all on one side Mind, all on the other Body. When he sees a case of conscious insanity, a madman who knows he is mad, his line fades away from even his imagination.

The distinction between Mind and Body now to be insisted on is this,—that the former is connected with Soul, and so connected as not in our thoughts to be either separable from it or combinable with it, while in our knowledge it is both. Mind is mutable and destructible by material agencies, Soul is not. Mind is materially manifestible, Soul is not. We ourselves are the two together; yet how can the material act with the immaterial ?

But if Mind is that part of matter, or is involved indissolubly with that part of matter which a man in thought is forced to segregate into his own individuality,—if it is that part of matter which enters into the constitution of the man, what is shown to us of it is a very small portion either of Mind or Man. We can only see so much of it as is revealed in the mirror of language; and that much, while not all its length and breadth, is none of its depth. The province of Logic, however, is, in all directions, determined by the scope of language. Logic, accepting the limitation so prescribed, is careful, in defining the field of its speculations, not to pronounce any opinion on what may lie outside the area thus set apart.

I. LOGIC.—Logic is the name of the science, or art, or instrument, in obedience to which, or by means of which, we analyse verbal representations of mental affections. As a science, logic professes to give an account of the laws which words necessarily obey when they are used in exhibiting processes of thought. As an art or instrument, it furnishes, or is used to furnish, rules by which thinkers may be guided to the correction of inaccuracies of thought or expression. A book which gives an account of logic is called a Logic.*

---

* Compare *De Morgan's* Syllabus of Logic, Section 1st.

Logic has also been defined "as the science of the conditions on which correct thoughts depend, and the art of attaining to correct, and avoiding incorrect, thoughts"; and as "the *art* of thinking, which means of correct thinking, and the *science* of the conditions of correct thinking." Sir *William Hamilton* defines logic as "the science of the laws of thought as thought." His remarks on the terms of this definition may be summarised as follows:—1st. Logic is from the Greek adjective λογική, itself from λόγος, a substantive which meant, sometimes, "thought," sometimes, "the expression of thought." It was equivalent both to the *ratio* and to the *oratio* of the Latins. 2nd. Logic is a science, because it is a branch of knowledge. The distinction between logic as a science, and logic as an art, at best only amounts to saying that it can be viewed in more than one way; that it is a science when viewed absolutely, and not in relation to practice; an art when viewed as the application to practice of knowledge. Even this distinction, however, which distinguishes nothing, is

II. MIND.—What we know in ourselves we have received from without, from what we call Body; and that in us which receives we call *Mind*. The medium of communication between body and mind is furnished by the nerves. The nerves discharge this function by successive acts which, in their affection of the mind, are called sensations. The science of Mind is Psychology.* Logic is the science of Mind, only in so far as it regards mind when verbally manifested.

---

arrived at only by help of a wrong distinction of arts and sciences. Art is a *productive* habit, poetic, or *poietic* as the Greeks said, and is opposed to a habit merely of action, to a *practical* habit, in the Greek sense of the word whence we derive practical. Thus, ethics is a science with a practical side, but that does not make it an art as well as a science. 3rd. Thought consists of the acts of the faculty of comparison. In this sense, thought is a recognition of similarity or difference between the objects which are submitted to the faculty of comparison by its subsidiary faculties. Logic, however, has only to do with the kind or manner of this recognition; that is to say, with this recognition as recognition. Hence, by "thought as thought" is meant the kind or manner of thought, in technical language the Forms of thought, or Formal thought. Again, the form of thought, as the object matter of a science, may be either contingent or necessary; that is to say, either such a form as may or may not appear, or such as must appear. Logic has only to do with the form of thought that must appear, that is, with necessary forms of thought. But the necessary forms of thought must be those which are determined by the nature of the thinking subject itself, which therefore are not acquired but original, which therefore are universally operative, and, consequently, are the *laws* or *conditions* of thought.

* Psychology has been described to be the Phænomenology of Mind; to treat of certain phenomena called mental, which are conceived to establish the existence and describe the nature of an immaterial mind. It seems hard to distinguish it as a real science from that portion of physiology which treats of man's nervous system.

III. Thought.—Mental affections* capable of being expressed by words, or other signs, or which are actually thus expressed to the consciousness of the individual affected, are thought.†

IV. Nervous Action.‡—It has been said that what we know comes from without to the mind, and that it comes to us by means of *nervous action*. In its simplest form, the nervous action of animals consists of an interchange of action between two sorts of nerves ; to one of which sorts we may, so far as our knowledge goes, refer every nerve. A nerve is either afferent or efferent. An afferent nerve, by transmission of an external force, is the cause to an animal of an internal affection ; an efferent nerve carries outward again to the ex-

---

* Note that bodily affections are also capable of being expressed by signs.

† The hypothesis of the text is not intended to contradict, and does not contradict, the existence of volition. Nothing but experiment can show that any particular phenomenon is an act of volition : many phenomena, once thought to be acts of volition, experiment has shown to be independent of volition: of very few phenomena would it be possible to say that experiment had shown them to be acts of pure volition, undetermined by aught else.

‡ In this and the following sections, no attempt is made to introduce more of the results of physiology than is absolutely necessary to give a meaning to the word sensation. Much is nevertheless owing to Professor *Huxley's* "Elementary Physiology," to *Dalton's* "Human Physiology," and especially to the edition of Mr. *Herbert Spencer's* "Psychology," now publishing. The student may be particularly recommended to *Draper's* "Human Physiology," for some very suggestive and valuable remarks on the compatibility of physiological results with those of a non-materialistic philosophy.

ternal world what of the force brought in is not
wanted to sustain the internal affection, and in
this way is capable of exhibiting the internal
affection. In some cases of very simple organisation, the efference is almost immediately sequent
on, and almost exactly complementary to, the
afference. In those cases, nervous action might
be, not unfairly, diagrammatised by the capital
letter U, the downward stroke representing the
afferent nerve, the upward the efferent; the afference proceeding into efference without any
visible breach of continuity. The capital letter
V may represent the case next in order of complexity, where we find the afferent nerve merge
its continuity in a nervous vesicle, or a collection
of nervous vesicles, which we may call a nervous
centre; and out of which again emerges the efferent nerve (or nerves). And a still more complex case may be represented, still diagrammati-
cally, but more imperfectly, by the letter W,
where three nervous centres interpose between
the first afferent and the last efferent nerve, and
where we may distinguish the first upstroke from
the second, by saying that it stands for a centripetal nerve; and the second downstroke from the
first, by saying that it stands for a centrifugal
nerve.* But this last diagram is very inadequate,
since the connection between any two nervous

---

* So far as is known, however, the number of the efferent
nerves which may be excited, is not regulated by the number of
the afferent nerves which excite them.

centres implies both centripetal and centrifugal connections.

5. The *idea*, then, of nervous action, is simply that of afference and efference, as the idea of a railway system is that of trains bringing things and people in, and taking things and people out. But if we look at a map of England, we observe that the railways have a many great centres of junction, independent of and yet connected with one another, at London, Birmingham, Manchester, and other places, and that at any one of these centres there are trains that stop, trains that start, and trains that pass through ; with all manner of other differences between the various trains and companies. So, in considering the phenomenon of nervous action, while we accept the words afference and efference as expressive of its idea, we shall in its details expect to meet with more than all the complications of Bradshaw. Of these details it is not necessary here to say else than this,—that there are in the human body at least three nervous centres, practically independent of one another, yet connected, and in mutual relations of superiority and inferiority.

6. The nervous centre which is most comprehensive and elaborate in its connections and branches is that which is placed in what physiologists call the cerebral hemispheres. This is that part of the body which man is wont to associate with his individuality, and material injury or benefit to which he calls injury or benefit to his mind. And this is that part of the nervous

system in which structural complexity and obscurity is at its highest, and where nervous action can only be imagined by aid of the analogies afforded by less complex and less obscure nervous systems.*

V. NAMING.—The result of efferent nervous action which proceeds from excitements of the simpler nerve centres is muscular action of various degree and kind.† In the case of the

---

* In the five-rayed star-fish we have a separate nervous centre, or ganglion, for each limb, and its nervous system might be diagrammatised by five letters V, all with their angles in the circumference of the same circle, but with their limbs outside the circle. Each ray of the fish must be supposed to contain one letter. This, we are told, is perhaps the simplest form of nervous system extant as an independent existence.

† Here I must note some facts which may be contradictory of the hypothesis of the text, and which I owe to Dr. *Hughlings Jackson*, whose special writings on the subject are named in another note. While all language is placed by the text on the same level, it appears that disease of a particular part of the brain may induce partial or complete defect of what is intelligibly distinguished by Dr. *Hughlings Jackson* as *intellectual* language, and not cause corresponding defect of *emotional* or *interjectional* language. The typical patient in this disease misuses words, or cannot use words at all, to express his thoughts; nor can he express his thoughts by writing, or by any signs sufficiently elaborate to serve instead of vocal or written words; nor can he read books for himself. But he can smile, laugh, cry, sing, and employ rudimentary signs of gesticulation. So far as these means of communication serve, therefore, he is able to exhibit his feelings to those around him. He can copy writing placed before him, and, even without the aid of a copy, sign his own name. He understands what is said to him, is capable of being interested in books which are read to him, and remembers incidents of tales. Sometimes he is able to utter a word or

cerebral hemispheres, the result seems to be *naming*. When, from whatever cause, an afferent nerve—either directly, by itself, or indirectly, by means of more or fewer centripetal and centrifugal nerves—communicates its own excitement to the organisation of the cerebral hemispheres, the complementary efference throws a motor or-

---

words, which he cannot vary, and which he must utter if he speak at all, no matter on what occasion. When excited, he can swear, and even use elaborate formulæ of swearing (as, for example, "God bless my life,") which have come by use and wont to be of only interjectional value. But he cannot repeat such words and phrases at his own wish or the desire of others. And as he is able to copy writing, so he can, when circumstances dictate, as it were, to him, give utterance to phrases of more special applicability. Thus, a child being in danger of falling, one speechless patient, a woman, was surprised into exclaiming, "Take care." But in this, as in every modern case, the patient remains perfectly incompetent to repeat at pleasure the phrase he has just used so appropriately and has so distinctly uttered.

It would seem that the part of the brain affected in such cases, is that which is susceptible of education to language, and which has been, after the birth of the patient, so educated. The effect of the disease, in relation to speech, is to leave the patient as if he had never been educated at all to language, and had been born without the power of being so educated.

The disease in question is an affection of but one side, the left side of the brain. This fact, coupled with the undoubted observation that speech is an acquired faculty, has led some physiologists to suppose that but one side of the brain is educated to speech. The left side of the brain governs the right side of the body, and hence it has been said that most people are born "left-brained," just as most people are born "right-handed." Dr. *Hughlings Jackson*, however, is of opinion that both sides of the brain are educated to speech, and that, in the disease under remark, the patient is speechless, but not wordless: his defect is an inability to reproduce voluntarily the most special of the acquired processes of speech.

ganisation into activity, which results either in
language, or, if, from whatever cause, arrested
before it reaches the stage of language, in something which is so far an equivalent to language,
as to in turn become, like language itself, a cause
of afferent nervous action. This efferent motor
activity, either in its more incipient stage, which
is *thought*, or its complete phase, which is *language*,*
we will call in its simplest act, *naming*. *Naming*,
therefore, is an indication or exhibition of a dis-
turbance or decomposition which has been excited
in the hemispherical nervous centre by the action,
more or less complicated, of afferent or centripetal
nerves.†

---

* The relation here hypothetised may be taken to explain the
generally admitted connection of thought with language, even
in cases where no voice, or writing, and little or no imagination
of words are present in sense or consciousness with thought.
And, taken in connection with what is said elsewhere in the text,
it may also explain how men can make and use a name long
before they can give a clear account of its meaning. Thus, in
Sir *W. Hamilton*, St. Augustine says, " If you ask of me what is
Time, I know not; if you do not ask me, I know." And thus,
Archbishop *Thomson* says, "The names we employ in speech
are not always symbols to another of what is explicitly understood by us, but, quite as often, are symbols both to speaker and
hearer, the full and exact meaning of which neither of them stop
to unfold, any more than they regularly reflect that every
sovereign which passes through their hands is equivalent to
240 pence!"

† One of the most recent observations of physicians is, that
disease of a particular region of the left cerebral hemisphere is
followed by a complete or partial loss of power in the naming
process, and by consequent inability to speak, even when all the
machinery of voice and articulation recognised in anatomy remains untouched. On this subject the reader is referred to the

8. The affection of the hemispherical nervous centre which is signified by a name, we may call a *sensation*. And as Mind, if not necessarily to be identified with that nervous centre, at least is in a connection with it, which is like that of a body of railway proprietors to a railway, and is only terminable by death (also, perhaps, by insanity), we may conveniently describe a sensation as a mental affection.

VI. SENSATIONS.* — A sensation is a mental state induced by the action, mediate or immediate, of one or more afferent nerves, and signified by the consequent reflex excitement of one or more efferent nerves.† It is not necessarily a momentary affection of mind. Its duration varies, it would seem, according to the degree of nervous force employed in its production. By the duration of a sensation is meant the length of

---

footnote on the first sentence of this paragraph, to Dr. *Hughlings Jackson's* "Physiology and Pathology of Language" (in the press; Churchill, London,) and to the same author's papers in the "Medical Times and Gazette" for December 14, and December 21, 1867. I gladly take this opportunity of acknowledging the assistance I have derived from the suggestions and directions which Dr. *Hughlings Jackson* has given me in matters of physiology.

* Sensation was defined by *Dugald Stewart* as the " change in the state of mind which is produced by an impression upon an organ of sense, of which change we can conceive the mind to be conscious, without any knowledge of external objects."

† The text, it may be observed, does not assert that every affection of every afferent nerve induces a particular mental state.

time for which, in any individual case, it may
continue to form a part of the human organisation. Sensations may be repeated or re-excited.
A sensation may be repeated by a repetition of
its original cause. As a tuning-fork may be set
vibrating, if its own particular note, or one har-
monic with it, be sounded in its neighbourhood,
so a sensation may be re-excited by the repetition
or the re-excitement of the sensation next after
or next before it in order of time. In other
words, " if any two mental states be called up
together, or in succession, with due frequency
and vividness, the subsequent production of one
of them will suffice to call up the other, and that
whether we desire it or not."*

10. Of those sensations which are distinguished
by names, few are simple or elementary, though
many, if not all, appear on first impression to be
simple. To draw the finger along a table† gives
a sensation which might appear to be simple, but
which is certainly to be resolved into the following
elements :—

  i. A sensation of time.
  ii. A sensation of contact.
  iii. A sensation of muscular action.
  iv. Re-excitement of former related sensa-
    tions, and of the relations of those sen-

---

* From Professor *Huxley*. What are called phenomena of
memory, and, probably, those phenomena also which are termed
acts of judgment and imagination, seem to be wholly or partially
constituted by re-excitements of sensations.
† From Professor *Huxley*.

sations, severally and collectively, to the present sensation.

v. Re-excitement of sensations not formerly related in knowledge, and of their relations with the present excited relation.

VII. COMPOUND SENSATIONS.—The same sensations are so often repeated and re-excited in the same mutual adjacencies of time, as commonly to come to be regarded as forming, collectively, separate and independent existencies, of which the corporated integrity is generally the first fact recognised by the mind, and is ever after regarded as the principal fact. That is to say, the compound sensation is at first taken for a simple sensation, as the Cathedral of Glasgow was supposed by the St. Kilda islander to be a *rock holluwed out.* And even afterwards, when the compound nature of the collective sensation is discovered, its individual integrity is still strongly emphasised in consciousness. Men call their consciousness of its integral individuality a *perception,** and they

---

* " The word Perception expresses the knowledge we obtain, by means of sensations, of the qualities of matter." *Dugald Stewart apud* Dean *Mansel.* Other definitions of perception are that " it is the apprehension through sense of external things," and that it is "an apprehension of the relations of sensations to one another," or "a discerning of the relation or relations between states of consciousness." (See *Herbert Spencer's* " Psychology.") The perception of an object has been called also an *Intuition,* so far as it is an act of the mind. Its product, in the same system of language, is a *Presentation* or *Cognition* or a *Singular Representation.*

suppose the several causes of its different composing sensations to be qualities inherent in some
material existency which is independent of, but
analogous to, the human individuality, and which
is accordingly distinguished as a body or thing.
But when again, afterwards, on further repetition
of the compound sensation, they discover that it
encloses another compound sensation, its kernel
as it were, which is also the kernel of other
similarly inclusive compound sensations, they find
themselves unable to give this compound too an
objective reality of the same description with that
of the former. They cannot call it a body or
thing, because, although, on the one hand, it remains still one and the same sensation, on the
other hand, they find it repeated in more than one
body or thing, and never find it isolated and un-
compounded with other sensations. Thus, Sir
William Hamilton says, " Let B, C and D represent a series of individual objects which all agree
in possessing the resembling attributes of *y, y, y,*
and severally differ, in each respectively possessing
the non-resembling attributes *i, o, u.* * * * The
qualities expressed by *y, y, y,* determine in us
cognitive energies," cause in us such and such
sensations, " which *we are unable to distinguish,*
and which *we therefore consider as the same.*" This
fact, however, does not make men reconsider
their hypothesis of the cause of the larger compound sensation, of the B, or C, or D. They
refuse to say that they know the smaller sensation, the *y,* in the same way that they know the

larger, the B, or C, or D. Calling it a *concept*, a *notion*, or an *idea*, they deny that it has any independent and absolute existence as an object of thought at all. " It is not cognizable in itself." Its existence is only relative.* At the same time, they describe this non-cognizable non-existent, as a mental fact, internal, subjective to the man, as opposed to the body or the thing which they call a material fact, external and objective to the man. But on the hypothesis of this book, things and bodies, no less than concepts and ideas, are called mental objects, seeing that they are all alike groups of sensations, or compound sensations, of each of which the component parts are mutually bound together by the one relation of adjacency of time. In space these different groups of sensations are, neither bodies nor concepts, mutually independent and distinct, for they all repeat, more or less identically, the same elements. Their mode of composition is not strictly analogous to that of their representatives in language. For although names repeat more or less the same letters and syllables, these letters

---

* Sir *W. Hamilton* thus negatively describes it—" We cannot figure in imagination any object adequate to the general notion or term man ; for the man to be here imagined must be neither tall nor short, neither fat nor lean, neither black nor white, neither man nor woman, neither young nor old, *but all and yet none of these at once.*" With the exception of the italicised words, this description is a faithful account of the facts considered in the text. The groups of sensations which are called by Sir *W. Hamilton* " concepts" are like certain chemical elements— they are never found but in combination.

and syllables are not numerically the same.   The
a in antelope is, numerically, one *a*; the *a* in
apple, numerically, another *a*.   Similarly, we
cannot strictly compare the grouping in compound sensations to the elementary composition
of chemical molecules.   The molecular formulæ
$(SO^4) Z^n$ and $(SO^4) M^2$ contain the same elements,
it is true, yet the atoms which are supposed to
constitute the SO^4 of the one molecule do not
necessarily constitute the SO^4 of the other.   But
as an astronomer, in his fancy, could arrange the
stars of the sky into groups on different systems,
so that it might be possible for the same star,
keeping in the same place, to be at once the nose
of a bear, or the tail of a lion, or the mid-blade
of a sword : or, as the same astronomer may be a
working member of this society, an honorary
member of that, and secretary to a third ; a
principal man in this social circle, a respectable
outsider in another ; a member of the Greek
church, but a subject of the British sovereign : so
one and the same sensation finds a place for itself
in innumerable different groups, in each of which
it occupies a different relative position, while in
all it remains unchanged and the same, relatively
to other sensations, in its absolute position.
In the words of Sir *W. Hamilton* :—" We are
conscious to ourselves that we can repeat our acts
of consciousness,—that we can think the same
thought over and over.   This act, or this thought,
is always in reality the same, though manifested
at different times : for no one can imagine that in

the repetition of the one and the same thought, he has a plurality of thoughts ; for he is conscious that it is one and the same thought which is re-peated, so long as its contents remain identical."

12. All sensations that are really compound but apparently simple, have, on repetition or re-excitement, a tendency to resolve, to become more distinct. Their individual elements, more or fewer of them, begin to individually assert them-selves ; and the sensation which, before, was in knowledge integral, now becomes many—now be-comes a group of sensations. By repetition it is that a sensation is enabled to enter into more groups than one, and that the intricate combinations ex-hibited in language are made possible. But to the mind, as a body of sensation, language is a gar-ment which is some times scanty, and sometimes voluminous. These sensations have more than one name a-piece, those no name at all. Some-times a sensation gets so identified with a particu-lar relation, as to lose in repetition its own identity, and its name in that relation loses all absolute meaning ; in other relations it still retains an independent existence to the consciousness, and its name has again a separate meaning assigned to it, or, perhaps, is duplicated by, or abandoned for, another, possibly more significant, name.

> There's an ocean round our words
> That overflows and drowns them.
> *   *   *   *
> Speech is but broken light upon the depths of the unbroken.*

---

* *George Eliot's* " Spanish Gipsy."

C

13. The complications thus occasioned, though considerable, would not by themselves be so intricate as they become in result of another fact. All sensations (there might be reason for adding, and the names* of some sensations) become, for a greater or less extent of time, a physical part of the human organisation. This many of them begin to be at such an early date in life, some probably before actual birth, and continue to be to such a late date, possibly are transmitted hereditarily to posterity, that the mind presents no record of their first reception, and small sign of its being possible for a mind to have them not.

> Rarest skill that Pablo half had caught
> From an old, blind and wandering Catalan;
> The other half was rather heritage
> From treasure stored by generations past,
> In winding chambers of receptive sense.
> *   *   *   *
> Shall the mere curl of eye-lashes remain,
> And God-enshrining symbols leave no trace
> Of tremors reverent? That maiden's blood
> Is as unchristian as the leopard's.†

14. Such or some such mental affections are those that have been put apart from others, and called *innate* ideas. Nor is it wonderful, when the seeming random and fortuitous way in which sensations hit, as it were, the mind, is compared with the ordered mode in which the same sensations are exhibited in thought and language,

---

* That is, not as the causes, but as the products or accompaniments of sensations.

† *George Eliot's* "Spanish Gipsy."

that people should be inclined to think of the
mind as an active agent, and to figure to themselves
that Mind deals with sensations as a builder deals
with building materials. A builder takes bricks,
and stones, and beams; classifies and catalogues
them as convenience may dictate; puts them in
store for use, and from his store selects at any
time what he may want for due arrangement into
forms of building. So Mind is thought to recognise objects by means of *perception*; by means of
comparison and differentiation, or, generally, of
abstraction, to shape out from its perceptions *concepts* or *notions*;* by means of language, to classify
and catalogue the things which it has thus found
and formed; by means of *memory* to store them;
by means of *reason* to arrange them into *propositions* and *trains of argument*.† Of such imaginations
this book necessarily does no more than take note.
If all known of a kaleidoscope were this—that
from without came to it, at seeming random, bits
of many coloured and many shaped glass, and that
these were the same bits which, with the aid of
our optic organisation, we see projected in ordered,
various, and infinitely numerous arrangements on
the object glass, what room would not be left for

---

* In another terminology, *General Notions* or *Representations*.

† "The rude materials furnished by Sense, retained in Memory,
reproduced by Reminiscence and represented in Imagination, the
understanding elaborates into a higher knowledge, simply by
means of Comparison and Abstraction. The primary act of Comparison is exerted upon the individual objects of Perception and
Imagination alone."—Sir *W. Hamilton*.

conjectures as to the nature and the action of the
kaleidoscope! But the most ignorant of civilised
men has just enough knowledge to confine within
limits all such conjecture: there is nothing in the
kaleidoscope which he is accustomed to call life.
If the kaleidoscope had life, however, should we
then consider him justified in framing a *Meta-
physic* of kaleidoscope? Perhaps we might. But
the explanation which the optician now gives of
the kaleidoscope would remain unmodified by any
admission, if any admission were made, that the
kaleidoscope was alive. And so whatever hypothesis may be entertained of the agents which
produce what are called perceptions and concepts,
it remains that, so far as our knowledge goes, the
elementary constituents of both are alike, and are
bound up by a like relation. The same elements
enter by turns into the composition of a sensation,
of a perception, of a concept, and of a judgment
or proposition, and are in each case united by the
same mode of connection.

VIII. ABSTRACTION.*—Among those already

---

* Archbishop *Thomson* describes Abstraction as a process of five
acts:—" 1. *Comparison* is the act of putting together two or more
single objects, with a view to ascertain how far they resemble each
other. 2. *Reflection* is ascertainment of their points of resemblance
and their points of difference. 3. *Abstraction* is the separation
of the points of agreement from those of difference, that they
may constitute a new nature, different from, yet including, the
single objects. 4. *Generalisation* [without which, the Archbishop
elsewhere says, there can be no abstraction] is the recognition of
a class of things, each of which is found to possess the abstracted

mentioned, it is an important note of sensations that the same simple or compound sensation has the power of being a member of an indefinite number of different groups of sensations. The differences between compound sensations that, in this way, contain a majority of common elements, appear, in mind, only as results of the repetition or re-excitement of the several compound sensations, and of their consequent resolution into parts. A man, who is neither a huntsman nor a shepherd, sees a flock of sheep or a pack of hounds, and, if the animals are all of the same size and shape, knows not, else than numerically, one from the other. The shepherd or huntsman probably distinguishes each individual animal in the flock or pack from all the rest,* and possibly has a distinct name for every one of them. The reason is, that each animal of the flock or pack is represented in the mind by a group of sensations

---

marks. 5. *Denomination* is the imposition of a name that shall serve to recall equally the Genus, or Class, and the Common Nature."

* " The Laplander by long practice knows and gives a name to each rein-deer, though, as *Linnæus* remarks, ' to distinguish one from another among such multitudes was beyond my comprehension, for they were like ants on an ant-hill.' In Germany, shepherds have won wagers by recognising each sheep in a flock of a hundred, which they had never seen till the previous fortnight. * * *Verlot* mentions a gardener who could distinguish 150 kinds of camellia, when not in flower; and it has been positively asserted, that the famous old Dutch florist, *Voorhelm,* who kept above 1,200 varieties of the hyacinth, was hardly ever deceived in knowing each variety by the bulb alone."—*Darwin's* " Animals and Plants under Domestication."

which, while it contains very many elements that
are common to the groups which represent its
fellows, also includes comparatively a few elements
that are proper to itself: the group representing
the individual animal constituting in common
language a *perception*, and that which comprises
only the elements common to all the individuals
forming a *concept*. The constituent elements,
however, whether of the perception or concept,
do not appear but in result of many repetitions.
The shepherd or huntsman has had the advantage
of such repetitions, the stranger not.

16. It generally follows, therefore, that, in the
case of all compound sensations which possess
many common elements, the first result of repetition or re-excitement is the appearance of the
resemblances between the compound sensations repeated or re-excited. The appearance of the
differences between them will be a second result.
In other words, men begin by seeing resemblances.
Afterwards, they distinguish differences. Similarly, when we say that one thing or group of
sensations is *equal* to another, we shall mean that
more or fewer of the elements composing the one
group also enter into the composition of the other
group, and are, in our particular point of view,
the characteristic element or elements of both
groups. To say "this is *like* that" implies a
lesser but a still remarkable elementary com-
munity. But to say "this is *identical* with that"
can obviously only mean that *this* name is the
name for which *that* is a name. A sensation re-

mains the same sensation, no matter how often it
be repeated or re-excited. It is unaltered by
being added to itself, or by being multiplied into
itself. And whatever is done with it, it will still
remain as it was, and where it was, and distinct
from every other sensation.

17. Let us now suppose a man to have seen but
one large quadruped, say a dog, and to have given
it the name, Dog. This name will be to the man
the name of a sensation, which he may know to
be compound, but which he will certainly have
very imperfectly analysed. For, show him a
sheep, and he will call that a dog too. The word
Dog, from a *proper* name, as grammarians would
say, proper to one thing, will have become a
common name, common to more things than one.
If, now, an antelope and a goat are successively
introduced, they will be "dogs" also; but, almost
simultaneously, differences between "dogs" will
also have been noticed. Every time the sensation
of dog number one, dog number two, dog number
three, or dog number four is repeated, it resolves
into more elements than it seemed to contain
before. While some of these elements are repeated in the remaining compounds, others of
them are not, and seek for names of their own.
Thus, one animal may get the name of "the
barking dog"; another that of "the woolly
dog"; the third may be styled "the horned
dog"; the fourth, "the horned dog with a
beard." The original word, dog, will remain as
the constant element or elements repeated in

all.* It is called a *class* name, or an abstract name, the name of a concept, a notion, or idea, of a creation of the mind. The other names, so long as they remain singular—remain the names of individual animals—are called, in opposition, names of perceptions; of, that is to say, things external to us, but perceived by our minds to exist, and to have qualities which we may separately name. But the analysis we have been making in this paragraph does not suggest any such distinction. It suggests, on the contrary, that the supposition of the absolute existence even of this dog, or of that dog, is only a way of numerically stating the groups into which our sensations resolve themselves. This same inference is, at the same time, decisively negatived by the fact that we have no *power* to give any such objective reality to the contained group of elements which is common to all the dogs, although we have just as much *reason* for giving it to this group as we have for giving it to the group which represents any one dog.

18. The mental affections we have just been tracing involve what is called, in the literature of logic, *Abstraction.*† This name supposes that in

---

* *Brown* quotes from Captain *Cook's* account of a visit to one of the South Sea Islands:—" The inhabitants were afraid to come near our cows and horses, nor did they form the least conception of their nature. But the sheep and goats did not surpass the limits of their ideas, for they gave us to understand that they knew them to be birds." These same people, it appears, were already acquainted with hogs and dogs.

† Professor *Max Müller's* summation of the philological history of abstraction is, that all names may be derived or identified

the process which has just been described the mind is really an active agent. Comparing the four dogs together, the mind finds them to agree in certain respects, and to differ in others. It throws the different qualities out of account, takes them away, *abstracts* them, in order to concentrate its attention on those that agree. These it brings, in thought, together, forming a *concept*, or a *general*, or an *abstract* idea.

19. Another view * of the same mental process is more coincident with that which it is here attempted to unfold. A vast number of objects are constantly presenting themselves to our senses;

---

with roots which invariably signify a general, not an individual idea, originally expressing " one out of the many attributes of a thing; and that attribute, whether it be a quality or an action, is necessarily a general idea " (" Lectures on Language," Fifth Edition, 1866). That is, in the language of the text, the first names were names of simple sensations; a compound sensation was designated by the name of the principal or the primarily recognised simple sensation among those which formed its parts. Thus Professor *Max Müller's* views may be quoted in support of the hypothesis of the logic of names. He goes on to say—" The word thus formed was intended for one object only, though, of course, it was almost immediately extended to the whole class to which this object seemed to belong."

This position, and the hypothesis of the text, are copiously illustrated by Professor *Max Müller*. He tells us that " moon " means to measure; " sun," to beget; " earth," to plough; *pasú*, or *pecus*, to feed. " Rhine " means to run; *Gangá*, to go; " Indus," to irrigate; "name," to know. Compare also Sir *W. Hamilton's* dictum, " Our knowledge commences with the confused and complex, which, as regarded in one point of view or in another, may easily be mistaken for the individual, or for the general."

* From *Morell*, who gives it as a view of " several of the modern German psychologists."

the perception of these objects leaves mental impressions which continue to exist, though apart from consciousness, and which may at any time be re-awakened. "These latent impressions insensibly blend together by the law of similarity; and when a result is obtained, in which all reference to time and place is lost, and all memory of the actual objects of perception from which the generalisation takes place, we term this result a concept. Thus the concept, *rose,* it would be said, is obtained by the insensible blending of all our experiences of this flower, so soon as the varieties are all lost sight of, and the common similarity becomes absolutely predominant."

IX. CONSCIOUSNESS.—A sensation, it is said, is not necessarily present to the mind. The mind must be conscious of it, advert to it, attend to it, perceive it, before it can become a mental fact, before it can have a name. Sensation may, in some cases, be almost amounting to a pain when the mind is only beginning to take cognisance of it. And of the relation which so connects a number of different sensations that they form one compound sensation, or so connects a number of compound sensations that they in turn constitute as constituent elements one great compound sensation, still more complex than themselves,—of that relation it may be said that it is no sensation at all.

21. In regard to these interpretations of mental phenomena, the present hypothesis is this—that

the intellectual mind may be viewed as a sensitive surface, the excitement of which at any one moment can only take place at one point; that this excitement may be called *consciousness*; that any one particular excitement may be spoken of as a *fact of consciousness* (facts of consciousness thus being equivalent to what in preceding sections have been called sensations); that the human organisation allows facts of consciousness to be registered internally at the moment of their origin, and for a greater or lesser portion of time, remaining meanwhile latent, and not actually facts of consciousness, but still on certain conditions reproducible to consciousness; and, in conclusion, that the human organisation makes possible, by signs addressed to the ear or the eye, the external registration and exhibition of facts of consciousness. The following conditions or laws of thought may be deduced from, or reconciled with, these hypotheses. A fact of consciousness must be itself, it cannot be not itself. The sign A, therefore, must be A; it cannot be a sign which is not A. The first of these affirmations asserts what is called the Principle of *Identity*; the second that of *Contradiction*, or *Difference*.* Again, in respect of any fact of

---

* Differently expressed thus:—1. It is impossible that the same quality should both belong and not belong to the same thing. 2. What is contradictory is unthinkable. 3. It is impossible that the same thing can at once be and not be. 4. The attribute cannot be contradictory of the subject.

This law of Contradiction only differs from that of Identity by a negative expression. The law of Identity has been thus ex-

consciousness, A is or is not its sign. Between these two alternatives there is no mean; and the principle which declares this fact is known as the *Law of Excluded Middle.**

X. Grammar. — While the necessary instrument of thought is language, and language consists of words and their combinations, there happen to be many languages—that is to say, many co-ordinate and more or less equivalent systems of verbal combinations. A treatise which professes to give an account of one or more such systems will be properly called a grammar. To trace the elements of a language or languages to their historical origins, and to describe the particular forms which they take, and the particular arrangements which they are susceptible of, in time and in use, is Grammar.

XI. Words, which for Grammar are many things, are for Logic only one thing, Names.†

---

pressed:—1. Everything is equal to itself. 2. In the predicate the whole is contained explicitly which in the subject is contained implicitly. 3. Nota notae est nota rei ipsius. 4. Conceptions which agree can be affirmed of the same subject at the same time.

* This law has been thus expressed:—1. Either a given proposition or its contradictory must be true. 2. Of contradictory attributions we can only affirm one of a thing; and if one be explicitly affirmed, the other is implicitly denied.

† The distinction of parts of speech in Grammar arises from an intrusion of grammarians into the territory of logicians, so far, that is to say, as such a distinction in speech is supposed to involve corresponding distinctions in thought. The necessary

24. When it is uttered, a name, from a result of sensation, becomes a cause, and the mind is

---

existence of any such distinction in thought is denied by the theory of this book. Both logicians and grammarians have fetched their raw materials directly or indirectly from one and the same language, namely, Greek. From that language all the commonly—that is, the unscientifically—recognised laws of speech and thought have been virtually deduced. If any language has furnished exceptions to the laws thus made out, so much the worse for the language. It has been either dragooned into submission, or stigmatised as indulging in eccentricities beyond the pale of reason. Of this tyranny the most signal victim, perhaps, is the vernacular of England and America, where *Lindley Murray* and his crew of followers have been exalted into supreme authorities over the language of *Shakespeare* and *Milton*. The student will find that, within the bounds of English and Greek almost all the parts of speech are interchangeable in actual use. And within the four seas of Great Britain there is a spoken and written language which hardly recognises the distinction of case, and which places, or did place, the article, disguised to grammarians as an expletive, before prepositions and verbs. Professor *Max Müller* takes us further afield in the same sort of illustration. In his " Lecture on Language," (5th Edition, 1866), we are told that the Chinese language has, according to common report, " no grammar at all—that is to say, it has no inflections, no declension and conjugation in our sense of these words—it makes no formal distinction of the various parts of speech, noun, verb, adjective, etc. Yet there is no shade of thought which cannot be rendered in Chinese." No analysis of any kind seems to be required for the discovery of the component parts of a Chinese sentence. Thus, " the Chinese sound *ta* means, without any change of form, great, greatness, and to be great." That is, it is equivalent to all three English words. " If *ta* stands before a substantive, it has the meaning of an adjective. Thus, *ta jin* means a great man. If *ta* stands after a substantive, it is a predicate. * * Thus, *jin ta* (or *jin ta ye*) would mean *the man is great.*"

Again, " when we say in Latin *baculo*, with a stick, we say in Chinese *y' c'áng*. * * * This *y'* is a root; it is the same word which, used as a verb, would mean " to employ." Therefore, in

affected by it as it would be by any other cause of sensation. Names thus become creatures of the voice and the hand. They have attached to them histories and prerogatives, which open themselves to the grammarian and the philologist. They serve as elementary symbols of number, and so once expressed all that men knew of mathematics. Lastly, they are symbols of sensations, and as such demand the attention of logicians.

25. Words as symbols of number have not always been distinguished from words as names. The science of number is the evolution of the consequences imposed upon thought by the condition of time. The most elementary of these consequences, being exhibitable by modifications of names, have come to be regarded as inseparable from the import of names; and, as a necessary part, therefore, of Logic. It is a manifest convenience of common and unscientific life to use the same word to express both a name and a number. It is as convenient to do so in elementary logic as in elementary arithmetic. But as scientific arithmetic confines itself to words which are numbers only, so logic, if it also is to be scientific, must use words that are names only. In logic, therefore, "man" and "men" are, subject to the exception elsewhere noted, two names for the same thing—two collective symbols for one and the same highly complex and imperfectly

Chinese *y' c'úng* means literally *employ stick*." Of course it may said, that a change of position is equivalent with a change of form.

analysed group of sensations.* Viewed logically, the forms "a man," "some men," "the men," "all † men" are to "man" or "men" as compound names to simple names. The added word is in each case the name of another sensation which, for the time, enters into the group that, by itself, would be simply nominated "man." As x in Algebra stands for an unknown number, so a, some,‡ or *the*, stands for the unstated sensations

---

* Of course "men" may also be a logical name for the human population of the earth. Numbers may also have logical names. Twenty-five is the name in logic of a certain number. "Five men" is a name in logic of a body of human beings distinguished from other bodies by the name "five." In "He dealt the cards by fives," "fives" is also a logical name.

All numerical symbols are logical names, but all logical names are not numerical symbols. When a name is used as a name, it forms part of the subject matter of Logic; when as a numerical symbol, of the subject matter of Number.

† The student has his attention called elsewhere to the ambiguity of *all*, which generally means "each and every," but sometimes means "all taken together."

‡ "Some," Archbishop *Thomson* writes, may mean either " Some, we know not how many," or " A certain number which we have in our thoughts." The former meaning is the logical meaning of the name; the latter meaning it is susceptible of, as a pronominal word. Archbishop *Thomson's* example is the proposition, " Some democratic governments have ended in a tyranny," which he supposes to occur as a consequence of historical reading on the part of the enunciator. But the question would seem to be, not what reasons may have led the enunciator to enounce his proposition, but what he means to declare by it to the reader or hearer. As he does not mention a definite or " certain " number, he certainly does not mean to convey it by his proposition.

It seems to be a purposeless analysis in Logic of a proposition, which sets out as its object the *foundations* of the assertion, as distinct from the *meaning* of the assertion.

that must be added to those making up man, if an
individual man is to be denoted; for those that
must be added to express a perfectly indefinite
number of individuals (one or more than one);
or for those that must be added when a particular
body of men is signified, as in " the men who lap
with their mouths." Thus, " a man," " some
men," are compounded names. Each element of
each of these compounded names stands for a
separate sensation, or a separate group of sensations, and both of these elementary constituents
combine to form a third compound sensation,
which is conveniently denominated by the name
of these its parts. As these names, so compounded, are mostly written together, as mathematical symbols which numerically multiply one
another are written together by mathematicians,
we may conveniently say that they are *logically
multiplied* together; and generally we may treat as
logical factors any names, however connected,
which are intended to be taken together as being
severally part-names of the same *logical whole*.

26. English names may appear as logical
factors in the following forms :—

I. Noun with article or pronoun : *A man, my
horse, that house.*

II. Noun with adjective or adverb : *A bright
noon, the then king.*

III. Two nouns with or without a third name in
the shape of a preposition, conjunction, or inflection : *A man of war, a pen maker, yesterday's dinner,
brandy and water.*

IV. More or fewer of the foregoing combinations put together : *Thomas Smith, a heavy fat man, crier of the court.*

V. Verbal forms with or without other parts of speech : *To rain, a swearing drunken brute, Amanda trying on a new bonnet, a nascent virtue.*

VI. Foregoing combinations joined to sentences : *A straight line which touches a circle.*

VII. Combinations of words which have lost their separate significations: *Wood-cock, black-bird.*

27. To the last class might be added such compounds as " presence of mind." In all much-used compound names the words which constitute their parts have a tendency to lose their own separate significations. A sign of this tendency may be recognisable in the omission of the article, which is only prefixed so long as the separate words retain in composition their original meanings.

28. Logic not only combines, but dissects words into names. Signs of the possessive case, of the plural number, of present and past time, privative and strengthening prefixes, modifying affixes and terminations, are all, in Logic, names, equally with their several stem words. In this sense, Logic makes one word into more than one name. In another sense it does the same thing, by what are called *equivocal* words, as, " light," which may mean *lux* or *levis* ; as " dear," which may be *beloved* or *high-priced.* With synonymous words, again, Logic enforces the reverse process; "heavy,"

it says, is identical with " weighty," " continuous transition " it declares to be the same as " transition with continuity." * Similarly, it sees no difference between,

I. *If two sides of a triangle be equal, the angles at their bases are equal ;* and,

II. *In any triangle the angles at the bases of two equal sides are themselves equal :*

Or, between,

I. *If a triangle is equilateral, it is also equiangular,* and,

II. *Equilateral triangles are equiangular.*

Or, between,

I. $\begin{Bmatrix} For \\ As \\ Since \end{Bmatrix}$ *All triangles contain two right angles ;*

and, because this is a triangle, this also contains two right angles ; and

II. *All triangles contain two right angles ; but this s a triangle ; therefore this contains two right angles.*

29. In the same spirit, Logic demands general exactness from language. Meeting with such a proposition as—

All right angled parallelograms are squares or rectangles, it obliges the meaning to be made

---

* A *univocal* name is a name which has only one meaning. An *equivocal* name has more than one absolute and independent meaning. A *metaphorical* name is that which has more than one meaning, but of its meanings more or fewer are temporary and provisional, in other words *pronominal.* Thus, a particular part of an animal is always named *foot ;* the lower part of a tree, or of a mountain, is sometimes named *foot.*

independent of the matter by a more explicit statement, as—

All right angled parallelograms are squares, or, if not squares, rectangles.

30. And, similarly, it paraphrases,

1. *All non acute angles are right or obtuse ;* as,

All non acute angles are right and not obtuse, or obtuse and not right.

11. *The ground is wet because it has rained ;* as,

The cause of the ground being wet is that it has rained. And

111. *It has rained because the ground is wet ;* as,

The cause of our knowledge that it has rained is our knowledge that the ground is wet.

31. An interrogative pronoun is, in logic, simply a note of interrogation ; *i.e.,* a name of that about which a question is asked.* The English language puts the *character* which marks an interrogation at the end of the sentence, but the *word* which marks it generally at the beginning. In Spanish, the character is put first, as well as last; in Greek, the word is often put last.† These differences are only noticeable so far as they show the independence of idiomatic language, which is a characteristic of logic.

32. A proposition becomes a question by a change in the order of its words, or by a change in the incidence of its accent. Then the change of order or of accent is a logical name.

---

* *Latham.*

† And often in English as well. *This is what ?* is as idiomatic as *What is this ?* The first, however, illustrates better the force of an interrogative name, *This is the thing about which I ask.*

33. A *negative word*, or affix, again, is the sign of a subtracting operation which is not performed but only indicated. In " it is not so," the sensations defined by " so " are exhibited by " not " in process of subtraction from all sensations. " Not " is the name of a subtraction, which may be imaginary, and need not take place, in fact. Suppose it to have taken place, and then the form " not so " may stand for the name of the remainder. When it is the name, and is not standing for the name, it is no longer negative, but positive. In names like inhuman, immortal, for instance, the negative has lost its force, the subtraction by degrees having come to be regarded as having been effected, and its name as a sign 'for the remainder.

34. A *pronominal word* is a word which stands by convenience for another word. The list of such words in Grammar might well be extended so as to take in such words as " thus," " so," and " do," in many of their uses. In Logic, however, they are all names with provisional and temporary meanings defined by the context of the moment. If we said " swans are white," we should mean that among those elements which make up the compound sensation, " swan," is that element which we name " whiteness." It is a usage of language which imposes in certain circumstances a change of whiteness into white.* And the

---

* Compare the word *Concrete*, which is a term relatively applied to any one of a number of groups of sensations which contain, as a common element, another group of sensations. This common

cause of this usage is another usage,—the ambiguous use of the substantive verb. "Is" or "are" may express either nominal identity or logical relation between the names it joins. In order to meet this ambiguity, language makes a change, not in that which joins, but in that which is joined. Between these two sentences—

I. *A particular compound of elementary rays is whiteness;* and

II. *A particular compound of elementary rays is white.*

the real difference of meaning * lies in a word that is the same in each, "is"; which, in the first case, expresses a relation of nominal identity; in the second, the relation which one element in a group of sensations bears to another element or elements in the same group, by virtue of their being in that one and the same group. This relation we distinguish as the *logical relation*. In Logic, "is" is used only in this signification.

---

element may be abstracted from any of those which contain it. They are *concrete*, therefore, and it is *abstract*. In this broad sense the name of any concept or notion is abstract; that of any object, thing, or numerical individual is concrete. In a narrower but analogous sense, an abstract name may be defined as that of a quality considered apart from that which possesses it, as *whiteness*; while a concrete name is that of a quality considered as being possessed by something else, as *white*. But this distinction is merely a paraphrase, with something like logical language, of a grammatical distinction, which answers to no difference in thought.

* Supposing " white" not to be used for " whitish."

When Logic finds it to be used by common language in another signification, it can only interpret it by a paraphrase, as, for example, "James is," by "James exists."

35. If the distinction between a substantive and an adjective disappears in Logic, so does that also between a substantive and an adverb, a preposition, or a conjunction. In

The danger is very great,

the meaning of "very" is strictly provisional to the temperament of the speaker and the circumstances of the case. It means that the probability of the event, or result, to which the apprehension of danger attaches, is as much nearer to 1 than to 0 as the speaker (and the hearer in assumed sympathy with him) is accustomed to mark, or supposes himself to mark, by the word "very." In

The risk is comparatively high,

"comparatively" has also a provisional meaning. Although it explicitly implies the process of comparison, it also supposes a provisional standard of comparison. But in

The bill introduced by him was avowedly directed against the neutral powers,

"avowedly" has a positive signification, namely, "with an avowal that."

36. Prepositions and conjunctions in Grammar, like "is" and "do," are pronominal. Thus, "of" may stand for "belonging to," as, "the martyrs *of* the fight"; for the Latin *de*, as in "I could not sing *of* love"; for "from," as in

" orient hues unborrowed *of* the sun "; for " by,"
as in " Ye shall be hated *of* men." *

XII. NAMES.—A name † is the sign, token or

---

* From *Howard's* " Grammar of the English Tongue " (published at the Education Society's press, Bombay). The imper-
fections of language, so far as they are liable to affect the validity
of logical forms, constitute *Fallacies.* A few of the instances
commonly given may be noted here.

" To speak of stones is possible; to speak of stones is speech of
the speechless; therefore speech of the speechless is possible; "
where there is an ambiguity in " of."

" 7 and 2 are odd and even; 9 is 7 and 2; therefore 9 is odd
and even "; where there is an ambiguity in " and. "

" What he was beaten with was what you saw him beaten
with; what you saw him beaten with was your eyes; therefore he
was beaten with your eyes "; where there is a confusion in the
applications of " with."

" The people suffer from famine; you are one of the people;
therefore you suffer from famine "; where " one of the people "
is confounded with " people."

" All these trees make a thick shade; this is one of them;
therefore it makes a thick shade "; where the fallacy is similar
to that in the preceding instance.

" Projectors are unfit to be trusted; this man has formed a pro-
ject, therefore he is unfit to be trusted "; where the conventional
meaning of " projector " is taken for its etymological meaning.

" What is bought in the market is eaten; raw meat is bought
in the market; therefore raw meat is eaten "; where the first
assertion is imperfect, and might be repaired by reading, " is
bought to be eaten."

All such mistakes are to be guarded against, by making language state exactly that which thought presents.

† The idea of a name, as conceived in this Logic, may be illustrated by saying that it answers to *Leibnitz's symbolical cognition,*
as that is defined by Archbishop *Thomson,* who uses the following words:—" A name, then, employed in thought, is called a
symbolical cognition."

symbol of a mental idea, concept or notion ; or of a sensation, or a feeling or perception ; of some impression or impressions that have been so made on our sense, as to be felt or perceived by the mind to form one whole.* When this sensation is simple, indivisible to the mind, its name, if it have one, is necessarily a simple name. When it is compound, is in fact not one sensation, but many, so that the mind may verbally exhibit more or fewer of these sensations; the name may be a simple or a compound name, may, either, by a simple form, collectively designate the various simple sensations which make up the compound sensation, or by a complex form designate in detail the same compound sensation; the complex form consisting of more or fewer of the names themselves of the constituent sensations. In the former case the name may be called a simple name, in the latter a compound name; but in each the name, as a name, is what it is in the other case. Many compound sensations have two names—one a simple name and the other a compound name. Ofttimes a compound sensation has no simple name, but can only be denominated, imperfectly denominated, by a name composed of the names of its parts.

---

* Or a name may be defined as standing for a "thing," and a "thing" as "a simple or compound fact of consciousness." In what follows of the text, the words idea, concept, notion, feeling, perception, or any one of them, may be substituted, at pleasure, for sensation.

These gems have life in them : their colours speak,
Say what words fail of. So do many things,
The scent of jasmine, and the fountain's plash,
The moving shadows on the far-off hills,
The slanting moonlight, and our clasping hands.*

38. Sometimes the name of one of the parts of a compound sensation stands for the whole. Sometimes the parts are not distinguished, or have no name. There is, of course, no difference between simple and compound names viewed as names.† The elements of a compound name may be compound names themselves, and any number of words together may form but one name.‡

---

* *George Eliot's* " Spanish Gipsy."

† "When a language is transmitted from one generation to another, not merely the words, but their mode of connection, as sentences, is also transmitted and appropriated by unconscious imitation, and thus becomes fixed. The latter point is not sufficiently appreciated, though it is quite clear that we do not think in words but in whole sentences; hence we may assert, that a living language consists of sentences, not of words. But a sentence is formed not of single independent words, but of words which refer to each other in a particular manner, like the corresponding thought which does not consist of single independent ideas but of such as, connected, form a whole, and which determine each other mutually."— *Waitz*, translated by *Collingwood*.

‡ This seems to be the place for noticing the fact that logicians sometimes take the trouble of dividing into classes those things which it appears to them are capable of being named. Thus, Mr. *Mill* discusses at length the following division of things:—

I. Feelings or states of consciousness.
    1st. Sensations.
    2nd. Thoughts.
    3rd. Emotions.
    4th. Volitions.

XIII. Meaning.—The "meaning" of a name
is the thing or things for which it stands. Any
word which has a meaning, therefore, when it
stands by itself, and any "sign" whatever, is, for
the purposes of this book, a name.

> "Even your loved words
> Float in the larger meaning of your voice
> As something dimmer."*

40. All words, then, are names; for they may all
appear in the pages of a dictionary with one or more
meanings attached to them. Particles as—yes, no,
to, for, by—are, accordingly, names; and we might
describe a *name* as a sign, mark, or symbol which
represents to the senses what may not be, cannot
be, or is not, of itself apprehended, at the time,

II. Substances.
    1st. Body, or that which may be assumed to be the ex-
        ternal cause of sensation.
    2nd. Mind, or that which may be assumed to be the in-
        ternal cause of sensation.
III. Attributes.
    1st. Qualities.
    2nd. Quantity.
    3rd. Relations.
      a. Likeness, unlikeness.
      b. Nearness, distance.
      c. Succession, concurrence, precession.
      d. Being greater than, equal to, less than.
      e. Cause, effect.
      f. Etc., etc.

Such classes of things are known in logical literature as *categories*, a word which literally signifies *accusations*, and which has
been transferred to logic in the sense of *predications*. The
doctrine of categories has always been considered extra logical.

* *George Eliot's* " Spanish Gipsy."

by the sense.* Names may thus stand for sensations which are not in effect repeated or re-
excited at the moment of utterance, or which
have already become parts of the human organisation.

41. It is possible for some compounded sensations
to have become so integrated, as it were, with the
physical system as to lose in consciousness their
compound character. In such a case the separate
names of the compounded sensations will also
have lost their force as symbols of distinct things.
But here to the aid of the logician comes the
philologist. The history of language shows that
before the integrating process had set in, or before
it had reached its present stage, these very same
words were in use, with very definite meanings
attached.

42. When the meaning of a name consists of
many parts, more or fewer of which have their
own names, as in the case of the simple name of
a compound sensation, the names of the sensations
so compounded, or the compounded sensations
themselves, are called by logicians *attributes*.
These attributes may be thought of as the marks
of the group of things which is signified under
that simple name of which, collectively, their

---

* "Jump," says the shepherd to his dog, and the dog knows
that this vocal articulation orders him to make a given muscular
effort. The man has *spoken* to the dog. During the night some
one opens the gate of the farmyard, and the watchdog barks; he
thus *tells* his master that something unusual is happening."—
Pouchet, translated by *Beavan*.

particular names express the meaning. And collectively, also, these particular names constitute to logicians the *connotation*, the *comprehension*, or the *intension* of that simple name.

43. To set forth the meaning of a name in terms, is to *define* it. When thus set forth, the meaning is called a *definition*.* As sensations in repetition or re-excitement tend to resolve themselves, the meanings of their original names are, in the course of time and discovery, liable to be extended, and their definitions, therefore, being expressed in words, to become, in a sense, incomplete. But as long as the definition is sufficient, in view of the purpose in hand, for marking off what the name defined stands for from other things, it ought to be held to be a competent definition. Thus, "Man is a rational animal," will remain a valid definition until it can be shown that some other animal is rational also.

44. When a definition is necessarily very temporary or provisional in its nature, it is commonly and usefully distinguished as a *description*.

45. In language and the practice of logic, it is allowable, for the employment of a word in any

---

* Sir *William Hamilton* puts definition under the wider term, Declaration, and says that a declaration is called an explication when it indeterminately involves only some of the names which constitute the meaning. It is called an exposition, when it contains several explications. It is called a description, when it consists of names which wholly or partially suggest only, but do not express, the meaning. Finally, in cases set forth in the text, under the head of *classification*, he calls it a definition proper.

particular chain of reasoning, to limit or even vary its meaning. Thus, for the purposes of science, it is possible to have names the meanings of which are exhaustively and exactly statable.

XIV. RELATION.*—Since no sensation can be repeated without a revival or re-excitement of the sensation or sensations proximate to it in order of time, no two sensations become facts of consciousness without a consciousness of their number; that is, of their sequence, of a fresh sensation—a sensation of relation between them. This being the one universal relation (we are accustomed to speak also of relations of equivalents, likeness, etc.), it has been taken as a sort of necessary factor to the connection of sensations, and as that which renders any two or more simple sensations capable of being related to the same group, and of being named under the same compound name.

47. As the distinction between the elements of a compound sensation thus appears to be succession, that between compound sensations themselves may be taken to be an interval or break of succession. This distinction is, however, a distinction of manner, not of kind, the relation between one compound sensation and its successor being in-

---

* This seems to be the place for noticing what have been called Relative Conceptions. A relative conception cannot be thought of alone, but only in conjunction with its necessary complement, or correlative. Such are *father* and *son*, pronominal names, respectively used for all groups of sensations which have certain common elements.

trinsically the same as that between a simple sensation and its successor ; and the foundation of the relation is evidently without the mind. Sensations come to it in a certain order; and this order is invariably maintained in all their repetitions and re-excitements, and constitutes what we call its *knowledge*.*

XV. PROPOSITIONS.†—The name of the logical relation, if expressed, has therefore the office of a copula or nexus between the names of the constituent elements.   It asserts that the names it is

---

* Professor *Max Müller*, in his " Lectures on Language " (5th Edition, 1866), says, " How do we know things ? We perceive things by our senses, but our senses convey to us information about single things only. But to know, is more than to feel, than to perceive—more than to remember, more than to compare. * * * We know a thing if we are able to bring it, and any part of it, under more general ideas. We then say, not that we have a perception, but a conception, or that we have a general idea of a thing. The facts of nature are perceived by our senses ; the thought of nature, to borrow an expression of *Oersted,* can be conceived by our reason only." Excepting, perhaps, the expression of *Oersted's,* nothing in this passage seems to amount to more than a statement of the facts discussed in the text.

† A proposition which must be taken for granted as self-evident is an *Axiom*. If not only to be taken as a fact self-evident for belief, but as a rule to be acted on, or instrument to be employed,.it is called a *Postulate*. If it is not self-evidently true, but only to be shown true by means of other propositions, it is called a *Theorem*. When it is of a complex order and gives certain premises (*data*) as the conditions of action (*solution*), which must result in a certain conclusion (*quæstio*), it is a *Problem*. When it is an immediate inference from another proposition, it is called a *Corollary* from that proposition. A proposition borrowed

interposed between may together form one compound name, or be together replaced by one
simple name. Such an assertion, taken along
with its subject matter, is what is called a proposition. In accordance with this view, a proposition may be described as the exhibition of a
compound name in analysis or synthesis.* The
enunciator wishes, by stating a fact, to ascertain
it for himself, or to demonstrate† it for another.
In the one case he may be said to construct a
compound name, in the other to dissect it.

XVI. The Copula.—In a proposition the name
of the connecting relation is distinguished as the
copula. In language the copula is sometimes
understood, but most often is expressed by what
is called a verbal inflection, or by the verb "to
be" in some one of its forms, or, where the copula
has to join compound names which themselves
are in the form of propositions, by such a word

---

from one science as an auxiliary to propositions in another science,
is called a *Lemma*. When it serves as an illustration only to
propositions of its own science, and is not a necessary link in a
main chain of reasoning, it is a *Scholion*. A proposition which is
proposed for discussion or proof, is termed a *Thesis*. When, to
explain certain facts, it is provisionally adopted as a demonstrable
Theorem, it becomes a *Hypothesis*.

* Compare Sir *William Hamilton*. "A concept is a judgment
* * * not explicitly developed in thought, and not formally
expressed in terms;" "concept" answering to the "compound
name," and "judgment" to the "proposition," of the text.

† A demonstration is the verbal exhibition of a mental affection.

as "therefore." The word "to be," however, forms the general sign of the copula; and, as a copula, has somewhat arbitrarily ascribed to it various significations.* It can always be substituted for the other signs of the copula.†

XVII. TERMS.‡—In a proposition, the names of the sensations between which the asserted relation is supposed to exist, are distinguished as the *terms*. These, in the typical form of propositions, must be two in number. For, as has been already intimated, more than one sensation cannot be exhibited by the mind without the exhibition of a *logical relation*. The mind can exhibit a plurality of sensations only in the form of a succession of names coming in pairs; the latter member of each pair being the name of the logical relation, and also the first member of the succeeding pair. The name of the logical relation, consequently, virtually becomes, in each case, a copula between the two extremes of a dipodium; as thus— $a\,c,\,c\,b\mid b\,c,\,c\,d\mid d\,c,\,c\,e\mid$ etc.§ Such a succession

* Namely, identity, accompaniment, sequence, cause, or resemblance.
† For "John runs," may be substituted "John is running." In the case of "therefore," the substitution would be less idiomatic sometimes, but equally intelligible.
‡ *Terms* are so called because they are considered to be the bounds or extremes of a proposition.
§ The dual nature of the proposition may perhaps receive a kind of illustration from the following newspaper cutting:— "He never could learn the whole lesson. In this instance he was unable to remember the third component part of gunpowder.

as the above is, in language, speedily transformed into a succession of triads; thus, *acb* | *bcd* | *dce* | etc., in which each triad is a type of the ordinary proposition of language, with its two terms united by a copula.*

XVIII. LOGICAL WHOLES.†—Sensations which

Whichever two he remembered, the third was always forgotten. His captain, attributing this failing to obstinacy, reported the matter to the colonel, who examined the man himself. 'What is gunpowder made of?'—'Charcoal, saltpetre, and—' 'Sulphur,' said the colonel. 'Now remember that, my friend—sulphur. Now tell me what is gunpowder made of?'—' Sulphur, charcoal, and—' 'Saltpetre,' added the colonel. 'Now, my friend, don't be nervous; forget that I am your colonel; think of me only as your comrade, who, slapping you on the back, asks, Tell me, old fellow, what is gunpowder made of? What would you say?'—' I would say,' growled out the soldier, 'that as you know it better than I do you are a damned fool to ask me.' "

* The theory involved in the text may be exemplified by stating that in the proposition "Man is mortal," it considers two judgments to be involved, having one common term, " is." With respect to the ordinary logical distinctions between terms, as, for instance, into singular, common, collective, abstract, and attributive, they are generally accounted for in subsequent paragraphs of the text. A *collective noun* is that which is otherwise called a noun of multitude, and is the noun of a logical whole which has been formed by a process of numerical addition. It is sometimes opposed to a *Distributive* name which is the name of a logical whole formed by abstraction. An *abstract* term is the name of a quality, considered independently of that which possesses it; as, " goodness ": an *attributive* term is the name of a quality considered as inherent in that which possesses it; as, " it is good." This distinction is grammatical, like that between *univocal, equivocal* and *metaphorical* terms.

† " Wholes may be first divided into two genera,—into a Whole by itself (*totum per se*), and a Whole by accident (*totum per accidens*). A Whole *per se* is that which the parts of their proper

E

by force of a mutual relation form one group, so as to be capable of designation under one name, and which can be expressed in this connection by a compound name, by a proposition, or by a series of propositions of which their names constitute the terms, are said to form *a logical whole*. If, then, simple sensations in logic are taken as analogous to atoms in Chemistry, a logical whole, in its simplest form, will be analogous to a chemical molecule. One definition of a *name* might

---

nature necessarily constitute; thus, body and soul constitute the man. A Whole *per accidens* is that which the parts make up contingently; as, when man is considered as made up of the poor and the rich. A Whole *per se* may, again, be subdivided into five kinds,—into a Logical, a Metaphysical, a Physical, a Mathematical, and a Collective. 1. A Logical, styled also a Universal; a Subject or Subjective; a Potential Whole, is a genus containing under it species, or a species containing under it individuals; and 2. A Metaphysical, styled also a Formal or an Actual Whole, is an individual as containing in it species or a species as containing in it genera. 3. A Physical, or, as it is likewise called, an Essential Whole, is that which consists of matter and of form, in other words, of substance and of accident, as its essential parts. 4. A Mathematical, called likewise a Quantitative, an Integral, more properly an Integrate, Whole (*totum integratum*), is that which is composed of integral, or, more properly, of integrant, parts (*partes integrantes*). In this Whole every part lies out of every other part; whereas, in a physical whole, the matter and form, the substance and accident, permeate and modify each other. Thus, in the integrate Whole of a human body, the head, body, and limbs, its integrant parts, are not contained in, but each lies out of, each other. 5. A Collective, styled also a whole of Aggregation, is that which has its material parts separate and accidentally thrown together; as an army, a heap of stones, a pile of wheat, etc."— From Sir *W. Hamilton.*

make it the sign or symbol of a logical whole, and anything to which one can give a name might be called a logical whole.

52. The different ways in which names may be used in expressing logical wholes are usefully distinguished by the employment of mathematical terms. The following compound name, for example, " The-tent-royal-of-their-Emperor," exhibits three names, (two being compound themselves), which are written together so as to form one name as one whole. The expression consists of a single term, of which the component parts are combined without any connecting sign, as if by the algebraic process of multiplication. The actual process may, therefore, be conveniently styled the *logical* process of *multiplication*. A further analogy between this logical process and its algebraic parallel appears in the fact, that, in both cases, the relative position of any particular symbol makes no difference to its value as a factor. The entire expression would remain unchanged in import if the fancy of the writer or the idiom of the language had placed that first which now goes third, or that second which now goes first. Another language might make "the" come *after* "tent," or "royal" before either, and so on. Thus Mr. *Morris* in his " Earthly Paradise" writes lines such as this :—

" Like the gold people of antiquity ;"

the equivalent form to which in prose English

would have " gold " before " antiquity," in Ice-
landic " the," if used at all, after " people," and
in Latin " of" after " antiquity."

53. Again in the following sentence :—

*The angles which one straight line makes with another
falling on one side of it are two right angles, or (if) not-
two-right-angles (are together equal to) two-right-
angles.* Considered as one proposition and relieved
of the surplusage of mere language, there are
four terms and a copula. Of the four terms, one
comes before the copula. Of the remaining three
terms, one is separated from the other two by the
intervention of " or." And the two terms left
are united by the word " if," which, being only a
sign of multiplication, has been treated as surplusage. But " or" is different from " if." The latter,
according to the account we have given of logical
multiplication, only stands for a dead copula,
represents a relation supposed to be already de-
monstrated, which is sufficiently evidenced without it. " If," at most, is like the sign × in
algebraic multiplication when it is written out,
and not understood. But " or," like +, is not
left to be understood. It expresses an alternative,
and the terms which it separates or brings together are in a very different relation from that
of logical multiplication. This relation may be
conveniently distinguished as that of *logical addition.* Very frequently it may be represented by
" and "; as in

Merchants are wholesale dealers and retail dealers,
[which we know to mean,

Merchants are wholesale dealers, or if not wholesale dealers (then) *retail dealers.*]
And as in

English Celts and Saxons,

[where Celts and Saxons are logically added together by the sign "and," the name "English" being logically multiplied into each of them.]

54. Logical addition should not be confounded with the addition of number and magnitude. Such addition is frequently expressed by "and," as in "two *and* two are four," "water is oxygen *and* hydrogen," or "it is brandy *and* water." This ambiguity of the word "and" in part arises from that general parallelism of the sciences of names and numbers which, we shall see further on, has occasioned confusion between *Classification* and *Logic*.

XIX. LOGICAL EQUALITY.—Of the various relations that in language may be represented by the sign of the copula, the logic of names only takes cognisance of the universal relation which has been already defined, and which may be conveniently named *logical equality*. This word "equality" is in logic a different thing, but not an opposed thing, to the equality of the sciences of Number and Magnitude. In logic, one thing is equal to another,* or, rather, one name is equal to another, if it may be taken in thought with

---

* Of course, one sensation can only be equal to another so far as they are both sensations.

that name to form, as integral parts, the same logical whole. The terms of every proposition, therefore, are equal to one another, the copula is a sign of logical equality, and a proposition is a logical equation.

56. In the case of *synonyms*, it should be noted that the expression of logical equality becomes an expression of nominal identity. When we say that plumbago is black lead, we mean to say that plumbago and black lead are two names for the same thing.

XX. NUMERICAL VALUES.—In English grammar a distinction is often made between so-called common and proper names which might be extended to all names. Every name in a language may be said to fall in one or other of these two classes,—the class where every name in one sense is proper to one thing, and the class where every name in one sense is common to more than one thing. The names in the latter of these classes may reasonably be called *common names*; those in the former, *proper names*; and that number of things which a name may happen to stand for we will nominate its *numerical value*.

58. Names which have different senses are capable of being in some senses common names, in other senses proper names. This is an affair of usage. Thus man in one sense is proper; it is the name of mankind. In another sense it is common, being indifferently applicable to every individual man. Viewed as being originally a

common name, the idiom of the English language provides two ways of using it, in derived senses, as equivalent to a proper name. "The" being placed before man, viewed as a common name, that name is made proper to some individual man; as, "I will kill *the* Man who breaks this law." * In the plural number, as Men, it again, viewed as a common name, is made equivalent to a proper name, as in "*Men* are mortal." And both methods may be combined, as in "I will kill *the* Men who break this law." It appears, therefore, that a common name may be used as equivalent to a proper name, or for a proper name,—first, by having affixed the definite article, which may be called a sign of the proper sense; second, by being inflected in the plural number. "Horse," for another example, is never, except in the sense of "horseflesh," used *as* a proper name. We do not say, "Horse is a noble animal." But "horse" can be made equivalent to a proper name. We may say, "*The horse* is a noble animal," or "*Horses*

---

* Other examples:—The Punjaub, The Doab, The Deccan, The Peninsula, in the English of to-day; The Bath, The Massachusetts, in last century English. As a general rule, when an English name of place or person is preceded by the definite article, we may assume that the name does or did connote something or other in addition to what it at present denotes. At the present day Englishmen and Americans, while they usually speak of "Hamlet" and "King Lear," as generally say, "The Medea," "The Œdipus Rex." Civilians talk and write of men-of-war as "The Arethusa," "The Bellerophon," etc. In naval writing the article is frequently omitted. The causes or explanations of these variations in usage are easily suggested by what is said in the text.

are noble animals," or " *The Horses of Arabia* are
noble animals." When a common name is much
used in a particular proper sense, the force of
usage and the course of time will often render
unnecessary the indication of the article. Thus,
we invariably say now " Massachusetts." In last
century they often said, " The Massachusetts."
Then " Massachusetts " was at least traditionally
a common name, having meant " Blue Moun-
tains "; and it was used in a proper sense, as
proper to a certain province. Hence the affixed
article. Now usage has turned the common
name into a proper name, and the article is
unnecessary.

59. A word may be used in any one proposition
according to its numerical value as limited by the
context, either for all the individuals it is normally common to, or for some of them. In the
former case it is said to be *distributed*; in the latter
undistributed. In " Men are animals," " men " is
said to be distributed; in " Some men are animals," " men " is said to be undistributed. In
both propositions " animals " is said to be undistributed, it obviously not standing for all the
individuals it is normally common to. But, in
the method of this book, " some men " is regarded
as a pronominal name; that is, as a compound
name with a provisional meaning, proper in sense
and distributed in logic. No numerical value
has been changed. Two terms have been multiplied together, and the result is a new term.
The same holds of all names which stand in

the relation to one another of logical factors. Similarly, the alteration of numerical value in the case of "animals" is to be regarded as a change of sense. In the one proposition, it stands for one thing, that is one numerical value; in the other proposition, for another numerical value; in each case its numerical value being determined by the other term. But the other term, scientifically considered, is in each case a proper name, though with a provisional meaning; and its numerical value must, by the definition of a proper name, be either 1 or 0:—1, if the name of a thing supposed really to exist, or of a proposition supposed to be true;—0, if the name of a thing which is supposed not to exist, or of a proposition which is supposed not to be true. As this reasoning holds of all names, for they may all be terms of propositions, it generally follows that the only numerical values assignable by the logic of names to names are 1 and 0; that all names are proper, and all distributed; and that there is no logical distinction between names as singular and plural.* Manifestly the same conclusions follow from the

---

* Except that to a singular name a plural name stands as a compound name to a simple, or as the name of an included compound sensation to that of its larger and including compound sensation. Thus, from Professor *Max Müller*, we learn that "man" in Chinese is *'gin*, and that "the whole," or "totality," is *kiai*. The two, added together, give *'gin-kiai*, the Chinese for "men." And again, *péi* in Chinese means "a class," *i* means "a stranger," and *i-péi* means "strangers." The English language gives analogous illustrations in words like "mankind," "Christendom."

definition of a name as the distinctive mark of one sensation, or one group of sensations.

60. It may be remarked that $\frac{0}{0}$ admits indifferently of the values 1 and 0. Therefore it would be admissible as the expression of the numerical value of a logical name, and would imply that that name was of indefinite numerical value. Such a name is "animal," in "All men are animals," for its numerical value is determined by that of the other term, and may, therefore, be either 1 or 0. Relatively to its original numerical value, absolute 1. it may now be any fraction of 1 ; yet whatever fraction it may be relatively and in form, that fraction must be absolutely equal to either 1 or 0 ; a condition satisfied by the fraction $\frac{0}{0}$. $\frac{0}{0}$ in this use finds an expression in the name "some," and "men are *some* animals" is accordingly a correct paraphrase of "men are animals."

XXI. CLASSIFICATION.—Coleridge asked his son why he was called Hartley. "Which Hartley?" said the boy. "Why, is there more than one Hartley?" "Yes, there is a deal of Hartleys; there is picture Hartley" (Hazlitt had painted a picture of him), "and Shadow Hartley, and there's Echo Hartley, and there's Catch-me-fast Hartley," seizing his own arm very eagerly. Hartley perhaps thought that for every separate word used as a name there must exist in nature a separate thing, and that the same thing has no business to have more than one name. We may suppose him to have gone on from this beginning to discover that there were more "picture people" in the world than himself, and that in the various simple names he had been putting together to form names of himself, all but the one word Hartley were common names. This discovery would have introduced him to the science of *Classification*.

62. Picture, Shadow, Echo and Catch-me-fast, are all names which, in the sense given them by Hartley, are each respectively common to more than one person or thing, and they in consequence require the addition of the word "Hartley" to make them proper names. By themselves, in Hartley's use of them, and as numerical symbols, they each have a numerical value greater than 1, the numerical value of the name Hartley is neither more nor less than 1.

63. We may also conceive Hartley to have extended his list, and to have consequently found words of a sort such that, while they are common to respectively different numbers of things, they are all, for a certain number, common to the same things. A series of this kind would be, for one—pictures, artificial-representations, works of man, productions generally; for another—echo, sound, vibration, motion; for a third—philosopher, man, animal. Philosopher and man are, up to a certain number, common to the same things; but, assuming that philosophy is confined to man, the numerical value of man is greater than that of philosopher; it is a common name to more things than philosopher is common to; there are some

men who are not philosophers, though all philosophers are men.   In the same manner, and on the
same supposition, the numerical value of animals
is in such a way greater than those of men and of
philosophers, that all philosophers are men, all
men are animals, while some animals are neither
men nor philosophers; others are men but not
philosophers; others, again, all the rest in fact,
are both men and philosophers.   Hartley, philosopher, man, animal, then, form a series in which
every subsequent includes, numerically and identically, its antecessor; the numerical value increasing
at every remove from the initial name, which,
its numerical value being 1, we may call the unit
term.   The end of such a series, (and every
possible name can be placed in such a series),
may be nothing but the boundary, in that direction, of language itself.*   After animal might
come living-body, with a still greater numerical
value than animal, but yet inclusive of it.   In
the same way, after living-body might come
body.   In the language of common logic the
denotation, or *extension*, of the names in the series

---

* "Thus proceeding, and at each step ejecting from the comprehension those characters which are found the proximate im-
pediments to the amplification of the extension of the concept,
we at each step diminish the former quantity precisely as we in-
crease the latter; till, at last, we arrive at that concept which is
the necessary constituent of every other,—as that concept which
all comprehension and all extension must equally contain, but in
which comprehension is at its minimum, extension at its maximum,—I mean the concept of *Being* or Existence."—Sir *W.*
Hamilton.

regularly increases as we proceed from the unit term.

64. Again, another fact to be noticed about the series in question is, that philosopher is not really the name of all Hartley, but only of what in Hartley is common to him and other philosophers. Man, similarly, is not the name of all philosopher, but only of what is common to philosopher with man who is not philosopher, of the human body with its living, sentient and reasoning forces. And so on, as we proceed in the series, we have to drop one part of the meaning of the initial name, Hartley, after another part, until we have nothing but body left, out of Hartley, as that for which the last member of the series is the actual name. To revert to the distinction of a previous paragraph, the last name of the series is that of the simplest thing, the first of the most complex ; the last stands for the minimum number of grouped sensations, the first for the maximum number ; and exactly in accordance with their respective places in their series, will the intervening names differ in the same relation. The meaning of each term in a series is thus less than and included in the term that precedes, greater than and inclusive of the term that follows. It is with special reference to this relation, the opposite relation to that of extension or denotation, that logicians call the meaning of a term its *intension, comprehension* or *connotation.*

65. To form such a series as the one we have been considering is differently called *abstraction*

or *determination*. It is called *abstraction* when, to make it, we proceed from the initial or unit term by taking away from the meaning of each name successively in order to get at the next name. When we proceed in the contrary direction, that is to say from the term of maximum numerical value, we return to each preceding name by cutting off so much of the numerical value of its successor, and the process is called *determination*.

66. The things to which any one name is common, form by that fact a *class*.* The series we have been considering may therefore be called a scheme of classification. In such schemes, the unit term — that is, the term which has unity for its numerical value — may be distinguished as the name of the *individual*.† The other names are *class names*; and of the class names, that which comes next after the individual is the name of the *infima species*, so called, because, according to the scheme, it contains individuals only and not classes. All the other species denoted by the other class names, do contain classes. The species named next after the infima species, in the present case, obviously contains two classes or species, namely, the infima species or philoso-

---

* The technical terms of logic, such as genus, species, etc., are called in the literature of logic, names of *the second intention*. The name of anything viewed as a mere existence, such as desk, table, etc., is a name of *the first intention*.

† So called because its numerical value 1 is not divisible in logic; logical *division* being the resolution into its parts of the extension of a name.

pher, and the class which we may nominate non-philosopher. Relatively to these two contained species, it itself is styled a *genus;* but relatively to its succeeding term, "animal," it is a species; and "animal" to it is a genus. The class "animal," again, contains at least two species, man and not-man. To them it is a genus, and in turn is itself a species to the succeeding term. This double character will be found to attach to every term in succession between the name of the infima species and the last term. As the series stands, Body, obviously can be a genus alone, and not a species. It is, therefore, distinguished as the *summum genus;* the other genera being called *subalterna genera.*

67. The series which has just been analysed is a typical series. Nearly every name, simple or compound, may be made the unit term of an indefinite number of such series. Every compound name may, in like manner, be made the summum genus of more or fewer such series, converging to it as to a common centre. Thus, a compound name may be the meeting point for an indefinite number of other series, each starting from an independent unit term. For example,

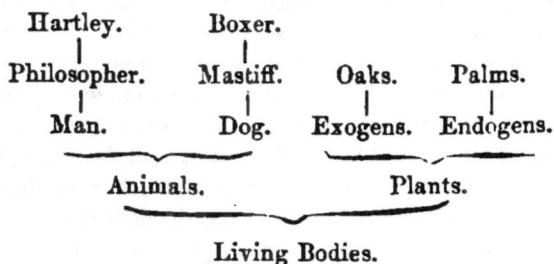

Hartley.   Boxer.

Philosopher. Mastiff. Oaks. Palms.

Man.   Dog. Exogens. Endogens.

Animals.   Plants.

Living Bodies.

68. Here "man" and "dog" are both species, *co-ordinate species*, of the including genus next after them, their *proximate genus*,* as it is called, namely, animals; "animal" and "plant," again, are co-ordinate to each other, and their proximate genus is "living body." That which distinguishes a species from its co-ordinates is called its *differentia.*

69. Classification, though a very important part of most works on logic, is not a part of logic. It is a separate branch of knowledge, a distinct science. The distinction, however, has not been recognised, and classification is so conveniently treated with logic, that the meaning of the name logic is most frequently wrested into an inclusion of classification as a part of logic. But classification plainly has to do with the matter of thought, as opposed to the form. Those, consequently, who limit logic to being a science of the forms of thought, ought to exclude classification.† Classi-

---

* The genus next above any given species is called *proximate.*

† The following description of classification occurs in Archbishop *Thomson's* "Applied Logic," and is interesting, not only in itself, but as illustrating the extra logical character of classification :—"A class cannot always be defined in words, so as to describe *every* species in it. From the lowest of its subdivisions to the highest, we pass through so many shades of difference, that we have a difficulty in perceiving and expressing the likeness between the extremes ; and properties which were prominent at the bottom of the scale, are in the higher steps forgotten, as nobler ones come into view. To distinguish the polyp, the lowest species in the animal series, from a plant, it must be defined as 'having a digestive cavity' ; whereas, the definition usually given for higher animals, and for the conception animal in general, con-

fication, again, implies that a name can have numerical values other than 1 or 0. It, therefore, stands outside the method of this logic, where no name, as a name, can have any other numerical value than 1 or 0. Classification, accordingly, is a separate science, as the science of names considered both as names and as symbols

---

veys that they are 'beings endowed with life and sensation.' Still we group them together by our perception of likeness; which, though not so obviously applicable to the ends of the series viewed together, and apart from the intermediate links, become so when we pass regularly along the chain. We might not be able to prove that the polyp had sensation at all, if there were not creatures a little higher in the scale of being, resembling the polyp in other particulars, and exhibiting more plainly the sense of feeling. We presume that it exists in the lower, because we see it in the higher, and though it decreases as we descend, we cannot show that it has ceased. The definition of a genus is the adequate definition of its lowest species only, since one which included any higher properties than the lowest exhibits, would of course exclude it. But in classification, the definition is not so much used as the *type*, by likeness or unlikeness to which we arrange the others, and assign them a higher or lower degree.

"Though the species in any great class rise by the steps of a regular arrangement, the same series must not be continued from the highest of one kingdom to the lowest of the next above it. The highest plant is often considered next below the lowest animal, whereas it is much more like, though infinitely inferior to, the highest animal. The animal, vegetable, and mineral kingdoms rather resemble ladders of equal height resting upon three different steps of a house, than ladders raised one upon the other. The lowest animal, the lowest plant, and the lowest mineral answer to each other; and the complex animal organism, the tall and beautiful tree, and the regular group of crystals, correspond in some measure at the top of the respective scales."— ARCHBISHOP *Thomson*, pp. 264, 5.

of number. In this view, classification is an important though not an extensive branch of knowledge. And it is necessary, as a part of education which the logician may naturally take within his charge, generally to understand the nomenclature which classification has introduced into literature.

70. The leading fact in the science of classification, is the distinction of names into connotative and denotative. By the *connotative* import of a name we signify its meaning, the attributes it implies or connotes; by its *denotative* import we signify the individuals, or classes of individuals, which possess those connoted attributes. If we consider the schemes of classification into which the names of our sensations arrange themselves, we shall perceive that in many the connotation or meaning of class names is indefinite. A sensation on each new repetition, resolves itself into new elements, and human experience, in many cases, has not yet completed this process of resolution. Thus it happens that, with our means, it is as yet impossible to exhaust the meanings or connotations of such names as man, sheep, etc. At the same time, the meaning or connotation of quadrangle, or triangle, is very definite. This distinction between definite and indefinite meanings is recognised in the science of classification. That part of the meaning or connotation of a class-name which constitutes its proximate genus, and serves to distinguish it as a species from its co-ordinate species, is called its *essence*. If, for example, animal

is a proximate genus to the species man, if the possession of reason distinguishes the species man from the other constituents of animal, then "rational animal" expresses the *essence* of man. The *essence* of a class name, therefore, consists of two parts: that which expresses its proximate genus, and is called the genus, in the case just cited, "animal"; and that which distinguishes it from its co-classes, from its co-ordinate species, and is called its differentia. What of the connotation or meaning of a class name is not included in its essence, constitutes its *propria*. A *proprium* may be defined as one of those attributes of a name or thing which do not enter into its essence. The name proprium simply means, proper to, and should, therefore, signify all those simple sensations which the resolution of a compound sensation into its elements may be made constantly to exhibit. As a consequence, those names which mark the *genus* and *differentia* are also *propria*, and *propria* may be divided into

1st. Those which express the *genus* of the name into the meaning of which they enter.

2nd. Those which distinguish the *species*.

3rd. Those which, constituting neither the genus nor the differentia, still always appear in the analysis of the meaning.

71. The analysis of a compound sensation will, however, generally yield elements which, or the names of which, cannot be considered propria, inasmuch as they are not found to be present in all analyses. In a number of successive repe-

titions of the sensation "horse," for instance, we may observe sometimes that the element "black" appears among the rest, at other times "white," sometimes both, and so on. Black, white, etc., are, therefore, not proper but possible elements in the exhibitions of the compound sensation Horse. Classification calls them *accidents*.*

72. The immediate application of the theory of classification is to *Definition*, or the resolution into its parts of the comprehension of a name, and to *Division*, or the like resolution of the extension of a name.

73. *Division* is part of *Determination*, in that it descends from genus to species; but its peculiar office is to divide the proximate genera of a compound series of class names into their constituent species. This process of division is partly arbitrary, and partly fixed. It is arbitrary, because the same name may appear as proximate genus to more than one system of constituent species. For instance, Star may be a star which revolves only round its own centre, *i.e.*, a star fixed; or a star

---

* A distinction is sometimes made between separable accidents and inseparable; those accidents which experience tells us are practically universal of the name, although no part, and in no visible relation to any part, of its meaning, being called inseparable. . *Black* is thus an inseparable accident of *crow*, though we may conceive a white crow; and although if we saw a bird in all respects like a crow, but white, and not black in colour, we should call it a crow.

In the language of Archbishop *Thomson*, "accident is a quality which belongs indeed to a subject, but can be taken away from it without destroying its nature or essence."

which revolves round a fixed star; or a star which revolves round a star that itself moves round another star; or a star which revolves round a point in space external to it. Or again, Star may be a star with rings and moons; with rings but not moons; with moons but not rings; or with neither rings nor moons.

74. In division, then, the selection of the principle of division, the *fundamentum relationis*, as it is called, is more or less arbitrary. We have seen that, in dividing "Star," the principle of division may be either Position relative to a centre of revolution, or Concomitancy of certain adjuncts. And it would have been possible to select other relations as principles of division, for many others would be suggested by observation. It is in applying the arbitrarily selected principle that division becomes fixed. The principle, once chosen, must be adhered to throughout the process. It would not be a just division to divide stars into stars fixed, stars revolving round other stars, and stars with satellites; for, to speak of nothing else, in such a division more than one *fundamentum relationis* would have been made use of.

75. Another condition of division is, that the numerical value of the constituent species must be together equal to that of the proximate genus. Practically, this rule is applied by asking whether there is in the genus any individual to be found which is not to be found in any one of the constituent species; and by applying a third rule,

which lays down that no one individual must be found in more than one species of the same division. A fourth rule, the completing condition of a just division, is, that every individual in the species must also belong to the genus. For that process of division, however, which is regarded as most purely logical, the first only of these rules is required as a guide, the others are only useful as tests. This process is known as *Dichotomy*, which means division into pairs of opposites. By "opposites" we signify the opposition between the members of a pair, like Policemen, and not-policemen. The second member of this pair may be again divided into a similar pair, as People imprisoned, and people not-imprisoned. It is evident that such a process might be carried on to an indefinite extent.

76. As *division* is a particular operation in *determination*, so *definition* is included in *abstraction*. The rules for performing it having been already sufficiently illustrated, it is enough here to simply state them. The definition of a name should give the essence of the name; nothing beyond the essence, and nothing short of the essence. The definition of philosopher, for example, should show that a philosopher must be a man; it should contain enough to distinguish philosopher from all non-philosophers, but it should not contain more than this.

77. It is obvious that a logic, which limits numerical values to 1 or 0, recognises definitions, but not divisions.

XXII. LOGICAL ADDITION.—The schemes of classification treated of in the preceding section, though they come within the plan of this book, diverge from its method, which, as said before, knows no numerical value of a name save 1 or 0, and, consequently, takes no account of what is called in grammar, plurality; in logic, extension or denotation. It considers a proximate genus as a physical whole—a group of sensations, and its division into the constituent species, therefore, as an act of what, as division, is technically styled *partition.** In other words, it reduces logical division to definition. Nevertheless, it finds an expression for the relation of co-ordinate species to one another; thus—

A mastiff is an animal.

A man is an animal.

A mastiff and a man are animals.

79. These three propositions are all independently intelligible and demonstrable, while the third can be made out from the first and second by the process of logical addition, of which *"and,"*

---

* Partition in logic is generally defined to be the division of the individual—of the unit term, in a scheme of classification. According to the logical theory which calls the unit term individual, this is impossible, and partition, therefore, is reckoned extra-logical. Logical division, by the same reasoning, and also because it is confined to the analysis of extension, is only applicable to class names. The division of an arrow into the point, the shaft, and the feather is intended for an act of partition; but the division of missiles into those which are propelled by mechanical forces, and those which are propelled by chemical forces, is intended for an act of logical partition.

and the plural sign are symbols. " And," it may be remarked, which here is a sign of logical addition, sometimes betokens *logical multiplication*; as in "Ammonia has-a-pungent-smell, *and* exercises-a-powerful-corrosive-action-on-animal-tissues."

80. *Logical addition* may be defined as the expression of a partition of a logical whole.

XXIII. LOGICAL SUBTRACTION.—As one group of sensations may be contained in another group, the expression of its withdrawal from the containing group would be a name for the sensations left after its withdrawal, and would be the expression of an operation which may be conveniently styled *logical subtraction*. The operation so indicated may be impossible in fact, or may be only indicated and not performed. Indeed, the logic of names can in no case have to do with the performance.

82. As an example of the expression in language of logical subtraction, we may instance non-philosopher. This is, in effect, the expression of the subtraction of "philosopher" from some group of sensations which includes philosopher, and is, therefore, a name for the remainder which such an operation, if performed, would leave. The including class is generally taken for the proximate genus which, in the case of philosopher, is man.

83. All negative names may be subjected to the same analysis as non-philosopher. Any group

of sensations, in fact, may be imagined to be subtracted from an including group of sensations, even though all we know about such an including group is, that if it existed and had a name, the numerical value of that name would certainly be 1. Thus it has been possible for common language to contain such a word as *nothing*. *Thing* is a name of that universal logical relation which binds up all our sensations into one logical whole. It stands for the whole of our knowledge, and its subtraction from something greater than itself is, therefore, both a numerical and logical impossibility. *Nothing*, consequently, is an uninterpretable symbol, and is used in logic much as $\sqrt{-1}$ is used in Trigonometry. The same mode of interpretation will explain *Infinite*.

84. It follows, unity being the most general representative we can have of the name of the including group of sensations, from which we are supposed to take the group signified by the given positive name, that, if any positive name be given, the corresponding *negative name* may be signified by the expression of the logical subtraction of the positive name from unity. Such an expression, be it noted, is not in itself a name, but used for a name—for the name which the remainder has, may have, or might have. A negative name is, therefore, a true pronoun.

85. Finally, it should be clearly understood that the operation of logical subtraction, as indicated in a negative name, is only indicated but not performed. To actually take one name from

another name is impossible; to actually take the numerical value of one name from that of another, both names being assumed to be names of realities, will leave nothing as a remainder.

86. It is perhaps, therefore, incorrect to say that a negative, (or privative) name is the *opposite* of its positive. In the first place, we have seen that it is not absolutely but only provisionally a name; it is an expression for a name. In the second place, looking at the components of the expression, a *negative name*, if a name, is a name which is not a name; and a *privative name* in the same way is a name, if a name, which is deprived of all meaning. The negative names in language may be divided into two classes : first, those which indicate the operation of logical subtraction, such as those we have been considering; second, those that are in reality positive names, as "unmerciful," which practically means "cruel." To this latter class Archbishop *Thomson's* instance of a privative conception, unkindness, would seem to belong.

XXIV. PREDICATION.—In any proposition, that term which determines for common language the numerical value of the other term, is called the *subject* * of that proposition. In

> *Men are animals,*
> *Some men are animals,*

---

* *Subject*, in the logical sense of the word, is by *Hobbes* made equivalent to *supposition*, or *hypokeimenon*. But it more naturally may be derived from its philosophical antithesis to *object*.

"Men" and "Some men" are the subjects of their respective propositions. In each proposition "animals" has a particular numerical value, derived from its place in that proposition, and different from what it would have if itself were the subject of a proposition. The term which thus has its numerical value determined for it is called the *predicate* of the proposition.*

Object may mean, first, that which absolutely is, whether known to exist or not; or, second, that which is only supposed to exist, and exists relatively only, that is, exists relatively to the knower. John Smith has an absolute existence as an individual man; as a father he has a relative existence, he exists relatively to John Smith, his son. Taking any object, that which is in it is *subjective* with regard to that object; that which is external to it is *objective*. Taking the mind as an object, an *act* of imagination is subjective to the mind; an *image* of imagination is objective. Taking a horse as an object, the horse, as existing, is subjective; as known to a man, the horse is objective. Thus, everything is capable both of an objective and subjective relation. And thus, as everything knows or is known, everything subjectively knows or is objectively known. Taking any individual man, to him his conscious mind, or *ego*, knows, and all other things are known. That, therefore, which resides in, belongs to, or is dependent on the knowing mind in general, may be generally called *subject*, or *subjective*; everything not falling under this head, which does not reside in, belong to, or depend upon the knowing mind, will be *object*, or *objective*. And by an obvious analogy, on the one hand, men have given the name *subject* to that term of a proposition which determines numerical value for the other term, finally ending by construing *subject* into a synonym of object; on the other hand, they have made *object* a synonym of *motive end, final cause.*—From SIR *William Hamilton*, in his edition of *Reid*.

* With respect to such a proposition as "No men are perfect," in this connection, the reader is referred to the section headed "Negative Propositions."

88. Generally speaking, a name may be said to be a predicate of any name into the meaning of which it enters, or with which it enters, by multiplication, into the meaning of another name. In its relation to any one or more of its predicates, again, any name may be called a *subject*. In a proposition, however, viewed as a logical equation, there can be admitted no such difference between the terms as is implied by the distinction of subject and predicate. But when a proposition is viewed as a sentence, the distinction becomes useful to the grammarian.*

89. We may avail ourselves of the distinction in *propositions* between subject and predicate, and of the distinction in *terms* between distributed and undistributed, to shortly state the common logical division of propositions into *universal* and *particular*. Those propositions are universal which have the subject distributed; those are particular which have the subject undistributed. Thus, " *Men* are animals," is a universal proposition; " *Some* men are animals," is a particular proposition.

---

* Of the relations between words which are named by grammarians, that designated by the word " predication " seems the only one which can be called a relation of thought. It is a perfectly universal relation. Thus, an article or a preposition is the pronominal name of a relation as predicated of a noun; an adjective or adverb is the name of a quality as predicated of a noun or verb; a conjunction, when used to connect sentences, is the name of a proposition as predicated of another proposition. And if the logical copula is taken to be anything more than a sign of predication, it must be taken as predicated of the subject, and the following noun or adjective as predicated of the copula.

XXV. PREDICABLES.—Any two names which may form the two terms of the same proposition are predicable one of the other. An adjective, consequently, ought to be predicable of its substantive.

91. It is a consequence of the numerical equality which is a property of logical equality that the terms of a proposition are mutually predicable. But as common language exclusively determines the numerical value of the predicate by that of the subject, not by a distinct expression, the terms of a proposition of common language, taken literally, cannot always be said to be mutually predicable, the subject cannot be in its turn always literally predicable of the predicate. In technical phrase, a proposition of common language is not always simply *convertible,* in fact, is never convertible, except when the terms are both distributed or both undistributed.

92. The same defect of common language prevents an adjective and its substantive from being mutually predicable. In common language, an adjective, as a numerical symbol, stands for more things than its substantive stands for. Its extension is greater. But the numerical value or extension of the predicate must be equal to, or greater than, that of the subject.

93. In the literature of logic, a *predicable* is a word that can be used as a predicate. There are five classes or two classes of such words. The five classes are an inference from the typical scheme of classification. With respect to any

two names which occur in a scheme of classification, and which are taken as the subject and predicate, respectively, of a proposition, the predicate must express either the genus, the difference,
or the species; a property or an accident. According to the more reasonable division into two
classes, a predicate may express either the whole
meaning of a name, or part only of the meaning.
In the former case it is a *definition*, in the latter
an *attribute*.

XXVI. LOGICAL MULTIPLICATION.—It has been
already provided that the mutual predication of
names that are written together, so as to represent the compound name of one logical whole,
may be distinguished as logical multiplication.
The verbal exhibitions of logical multiplication
and some consequences which come from it may
be here conveniently illustrated.

95. In "this hat is black," *this* and *hat* are
logically multiplied together. In "this is a black
hat," *black* and *hat* are logically multiplied together.
Generally, therefore, the names which form any
compound name, and which, consequently, are all
compredicable of the same thing, are to be considered as logically multiplied together. When
now a compound name is the name of a non-
existent—that is, when the names composing it are
the names of sensations that cannot come together,
are non-compredicable names — the numerical
value of that compound must be, as we have seen
in a preceding paragraph, equal to 0. That is to

say, the result of the multiplication together of
the factors composing that compound name is 0,
and the predication or predications which it implies are false.

96. The following examples, of which the third
is, by logical multiplication, a deduction from the
others, may now be intelligible* :—

    I. *Man is mortal.*
    II. *Man is immortal.*
    III. Man man is mortal immortal.

97. The subjects of I. and II. multiplied together are unchanged. A name multiplied by
itself equals itself. The square of a name equals
the name.† The subject of III. might be as well
expressed by "man" as by "man man." And
this is reasonable. For names stand for sensations. But a sensation repeated is the same sensation still.

98. Again, supposing mortal to be the pure
negative of immortal, the two words multiplied
together must equal nothing. For, together,

* It may be rendered more intelligible by the following example :—
    I. Honesty is deserving reward.
    II. A negro is a fellow-creature.
    III. An honest negro is a fellow-creature deserving reward.
The two logical equations, I. and II., logically multiplied together, produce III. The example is taken from Archbishop
Thomson, who brings it forward as an instance of "Immediate
Inference by added Determinants."
† In mathematical language, if x stand for the name of any
logical whole, then, $x^2=x$. The same follows, also, from the
numerical value of a name as the sign of a logical whole. Either
1, 0, or $\frac{0}{0}$, multiplied into itself, equals itself.

they form the compound name of a plain non-existent ; one of them is a false predication. Again, taken separately, both being predicated of the same subject in I. and II.; one must of necessity be a true predication, and the other a false one. Then the numerical value of the one, will be 1, of the other, 0. But these numbers multiplied together as numbers equal 0 ; just as we have seen that the corresponding names when multiplied together are equal to 0. Hence we may take as a rule, that a name logically multiplied into its negative must give 0 as the numerical value of the resulting compound name.*

XXVII. Negative Propositions.—The interpretation given above of negative names applies equally to negative propositions. A proposition is but a name in analysis or synthesis, and a negative attached to it which is to be referred not to the subject nor to the predicate, but to the whole proposition, merely indicates that the compound sensation signified by the proposition is to be considered as subtracted from a larger and including sensation. The operation itself, it may be remarked, is signified by the negative sign only, which in effect declares that the name or proposition to which it is attached, is the subject of the operation. In a *negative name*, then, the

---

* Numerically, this rule is deducible from the law $x^2 = x$, an equation which may be written thus, $x - x^2 = 0$, whence $x(1-x) = 0$. It is obvious that the rule, whether stated in words or in symbols, is only an expression of the principle of contradiction.

negative sign plays the part of an adjective, in a negative proposition, of a predicate. A negative proposition is not a simple but a compound proposition. It is a proposition which for a subject has another proposition.

100. This analysis of negative propositions is to some extent verified by the forms of language. In English, the universal negative proposition is idiomatically expressed thus—

No men are good,

where the negative is placed before the proposition as an adjective before its substantive, and, accordantly with the genius of the language, can be referred neither to subject, copula, nor predicate.*

101. In view of this interpretation† of a negative proposition, it becomes useless to dispute whether the negative proposition should be attached to the predicate or the copula. If to enunciate a negative proposition is to affirm a negative of an affirmative proposition taken as a subject, the negative proposition is only a complex form of the affirmative proposition.

102. In ordinary logic, the recognition of the

---

* So, in the common example, "All that glitters is not gold," what is meant is, "it is not true that all that glitters is gold." Those who virtually take "not" as part of the predicate are obliged to apply a *collective* in place of a *distributive* sense to "all."

† Countenanced, I observe, by the high authority of Mr. *Latham*, who "doubts whether it be in accordance with the phenomena of language to make the negative element of propositions a part of either predicate or copula."—Logic, p. 26.

negative form of proposition doubles the number of types. As there is an *affirmative universal*, so there must be a *negative universal;* and with the *affirmative particular* also must stand the *negative particular.** All negative propositions *distribute* the predicate. If we say " no men are innocent," we assert of all innocent things that none of them are men. If we say " some triangles are not scalene," we assert of all scalene triangles that they number none of those particular triangles that we define by the word " some."

103. Affirmative propositions, on the contrary, do not distribute the predicate. When we say " All men are animals," or "Some men are animals," we do not speak of all animals.

104. Finally, as the subject of every universal proposition is distributed (see the section headed Predication), and the subject of every particular proposition undistributed, it follows that the universal affirmative has the subject alone distributed, the universal negative both subject and predicate, the particular negative only the predicate, the particular affirmative neither subject nor predicate.

XXVIII. THE CALCULUS OF LOGIC.—We have seen that the logic of names provides for the expression of operations on names and of the uni-

---

* The attribution to a proposition of affirmation or negation constitutes its *quality;* of universality or particularity, its *quantity.*

versal logical relation between names, of logical multiplication, addition, subtraction, and of logical equality : that we may indicate operations on names that neither are nor can be performed; and that in all operations and equalities the names employed must each have for its numerical value either 1 or 0. These facts constitute the basis of Professor *Boole's* " Calculus of Logic," which may be defined to consist of the laws, the axioms, and the processes of an Algebra, in which the symbols *x*, *y*, *z*, etc., admit indifferently of the values 0 and 1, and of these values alone.

APPENDIX.

Mr. *Stanley Jevons* has published a work entitled "Pure Logic," which he, himself, characterises as being little more than an attempt to translate Professor *Boole's* forms into processes of self-evident meaning and force. The mention of this fact may introduce certain observations that have been suggested by Mr. *Jevons's* critical remarks on Professor *Boole's* system,—remarks which the present writer is the more induced to notice, because they constitute the only detailed criticism of Professor *Boole's* system which he has been yet fortunate enough to meet with.

Mr. *Jevons's* remarks are chiefly grouped under separate "objections." His first objection is that "*Boole's* symbols are essentially different from the names or symbols of common discourse,—his logic is not the logic of common thought." Mr. *Jevons*, in enforcing this objection, remarks that Professor *Boole's* symbols, in expressing this proposition, "A peer is either a duke, or a marquis, or an earl, or a viscount, or a baron," would necessarily imply that a peer can *not* be at once a duke and marquis, or marquis and earl. The answer is, that while common discourse can, but does not, express the compredicability of these various titles, it is a cardinal point with Professor *Boole*, equally with Sir *William Hamilton*, that everything implied in thought should be expressed by Logic. He would, therefore, before symbolising the given sentence, enquire whether the terms "duke," "marquis," etc., were meant to be mutually exclusive or not: it is therefore not strictly correct to say that his symbols, if expressing the given sentence, would necessarily imply that a duke could not be a marquis. Mr. *Jevons*, indeed, seems to think that such a preliminary enquiry is "consulting the matter," and therefore extra-logical. But until it is known what meaning he attaches, in this connection, to the phrase "consulting the matter," it is only necessary to say, that Professor *Boole's* logic is scientific; common discourse is unscientific, and leaves things to be understood which science expresses. But as the logic only pretends to interpret the discourse, this difference between them seems hardly to constitute an essential difference. At any rate, Mr. *Jevons's* objection is equally valid against Professor *Boole's* symbol for A, $y=vx$, against Sir *William Hamilton's* "all x is *some y*," and against, perhaps, the majority of logicians, who, if they do not name the *some* in A, direct the student to *think* it.

Mr. *Jevons* again takes the form $x = y + z$, and then calls x "Cæsar"; y, "Conqueror of the Gauls"; z, "First Emperor of Rome"; from these assignments, interpreting the form to mean "Cæsar is the conqueror of the Gauls or the first emperor of Rome." Next he proceeds to subtract z from both sides, getting $x-z=y$, and thus, with some triumph, interprets the result, "Cæsar, providing he is not the first emperor of Rome, is the conqueror of the Gauls!"

It is perhaps sufficient to say here that Mr. *Jevons* treats Professor *Boole's* symbols as he would not treat those of common algebra. It would be easy, by assigning arbitrary values to the separate symbols involved in a given equation, to deduce all manner of absurd consequences from their connection as fixed by the equation. Were the sentence "Cæsar is the conqueror of the Gauls or the first emperor of Rome," submitted in good faith to Professor *Boole's* system, the first question would be what "or" meant. Is it disjunctive, as in "saint or sinner," and in "saint or latter-day saint," or is it expressive of a synonym, as in "sleep or slumber"? If the former, the symbolical expression of the sentence "Cæsar is the conqueror of the Gauls or the first emperor of Rome" might be something like the form given by Mr. *Jevons*, as $x=y\ (1-z)+(1-y)\ z$; or $x=y + (1-y)\ z$; if the latter, $x=yz$.

In common discourse the same questions would have to be somehow answered before the meaning of the proposition could be considered to be settled. In this case again we find common discourse to be ambiguous, so far unscientific, and so far necessarily different from what logic necessarily must be, so long as logic pretends to be a science.

The second objection, which is that there are no such operations in pure logic as addition and subtraction, may be taken with the third, which is that Professor *Boole's* system is "inconsistent with the self-evident law of thought" in Mr. *Stanley Jevons's* system, a law which he expresses thus, $(A+A=A)$.

It is perplexing tó find Mr. *Jevons* first stating that there is no such thing in his logic as addition, and then, in almost the next page, using the sign of addition in enunciating his own "self-evident law of thought." It can only be conjectured that one of two things is the case,—either that Mr. *Jevons* uses the sign of addition where Professor *Boole* uses that of multiplication, or that he has omitted to take into account the import of the first proposition in Professor *Boole's* chapter of "Abbreviations." It may be admitted, however, that Professor *Boole's* phraseology does not always recognise the distinction between the logics of extension and intension.

The fourth and last objection taken against Professor *Boole's* system, is taken *à-propos* of the symbols $\frac{\text{I}}{\text{I}}$, $\frac{0}{0}$, $\frac{0}{0}$, $\frac{\text{I}}{0}$. Shortly stated, it is that the calculus made use of by Professor *Boole* is a system which only points out truths that, by another system of reasoning, we have to learn are certainly true. This objection, if subjected to certain modifications, has a justification. It need only be added here now, that whatever agreements or disagreements may exist between their views on matters of detail, the present writer cordially concurs with Mr. *Jevons* where the latter says of logic as it now is, since the appearance of Professor *Boole's* "Laws of Thought," that it "is to logic before that work as mathematics with equations of any degree are to mathematics with equations of only one degree."

INDEX.